Reading & Writing
Great Mayan Reef

NATIONAL GEOGRAPHIC
L E A R N I N G

Australia • Brazil • Mexico • Singapore • United Kingdom • United States

NATIONAL GEOGRAPHIC
L E A R N I N G

National Geographic Learning,
a Cengage Company

Reading & Writing, Great Mayan Reef

**Laurie Blass, Mari Vargo, Keith S. Folse,
April Muchmore-Vokoun, Elena Vestri**

Publisher: Sherrise Roehr

Executive Editor: Laura LeDréan

Managing Editor: Jennifer Monaghan

Digital Implementation Manager,
Irene Boixareu

Senior Media Researcher: Leila Hishmeh

Director of Global Marketing: Ian Martin

Regional Sales and National Account
Manager: Andrew O'Shea

Content Project Manager: Ruth Moore

Senior Designer: Lisa Trager

Manufacturing Planner: Mary Beth Hennebury

Composition: Lumina Datamatics

Student Edition: Reading & Writing, Great Mayan Reef
ISBN-13: 978-0-357-13827-4

National Geographic Learning
20 Channel Center Street
Boston, MA 02210
USA

Locate your local office at **international.cengage.com/region**

Visit National Geographic Learning online at **ELTNGL.com**
Visit our corporate website at **www.cengage.com**

Printed in China
Print Number: 02   Print Year: 2019

PHOTO CREDITS

01 (c) © Corey Rich/Aurora Photos, 02-03 (c) © Mauricio Graiki/Shutterstock, 05 (t) Adam Pretty/Getty Images, 06 (b) Bloomberg/Getty Images, 09 (t) © Brady Barr/National Geographic Creative, 10 (br) © Joel Sartore/National Geographic Creative, 12 (c) ZUMA Press, Inc./Alamy Stock Photo, 13 (c) Brian J. Skerry/National Geographic Creative, 15 (b) Fabrice Coffrini/Getty Images, 20-21: © Paper Boat Creative/Taxi/ Getty Images, 22: © B Christopher/Alamy, 27: © Paul Bradbury/OJO Images/Getty Images, 29: © Juanmonino/ E+/Getty Images, 30: © View Stock/Jupiter Images, 32: © David Sacks/Getty Images, 34: © Petr Malyshev/Shutterstock.com; Left: © Ciaran Griffin/Getty Images; Right, 35: © sjeacle/Shutterstock. com; Top left: © Frederic Cirou/PhotoAlto sas/Alamy; Top right:© Naiyyer/Shutterstock.com; Bottom left: © B. BOISSONNET/ BSIP SA/Alamy; Bottom right, 36: © Skylines/Shutterstock.com; Top left: © Aaron Amat/Shutterstock.com; Top right: © Daniel Kirkegaard Mouritsen/Shutterstock.com; Bottom left:© whitehoune/Shutterstock.com;Bottom right, 41 (c) Joel Sartore, National Geographic Photo Ark/National Geographic Creative, 42 (bl) Joel Sartore, National Geographic Photo Ark/National Geographic Creative, 42 (bc) Joel Sartore, National Geographic Photo Ark/National Geographic Creative, 42 (br) Joel Sartore/National Geographic Creative, 43 (c) Joel Sartore, National Geographic Photo Ark/National Geographic Creative, 45 (c) David Doubilet/National Geographic Creative, 46 (tl) © Mariana Fuentes, 46 (bc) Kent Kobersteen/National Geographic Creative, 47 (cr) David Doubilet/National Geographic Creative, 49 (t) Joel Sartore, National Geographic Photo Ark/National Geographic Creative, 50 (cr) Joel Sartore, National Geographic Photo Ark/National Geographic Creative, 52 (br) Ivy Close Images/Alamy Stock Photo, 53 (c) Joel Sartore, National Geographic Photo Ark/National Geographic Creative, 54 (t) Joel Sartore/National Geographic, 54 (bc) Joel Sartore, National Geographic Photo Ark/National Geographic Creative, 55 (t) Joel Sartore, National Geographic Photo Ark/National Geographic Creative, 55 (bc) Joel Sartore/National Geographic Creative, 57 (bc) Joel Sartore, National Geographic Photo Ark/National Geographic Creative, 59 (br) Joel Sartore, National Geographic Photo Ark/National Geographic Creative, 62-63: ″ PETE RYAN/ National Geographic Creative, 65: ″ Paul Fusco/Magnum Photos, 66: Source: www. unchartedplay.com, 68: ″ Hans Neleman/Taxi/Getty Images, 71: ″ bygone/Alamy, 74: ″ Paula Bronstein/Getty Images, 77: Top left: ″ GonzaloArroyo Moreno/Getty Images;Top right: ″ INTERFOTO/ Alamy; Center left: ″ Everett Collection Inc/Alamy; Center middle: ″ DeAgostini/Getty Images; Center right: ″ Toshifumi Kitamura/AFP/Getty Images;Bottom left: ″ Apic/Hulton Archive/Getty Images; Bottommiddle: JT Vintage/Glasshouse Images/Alamy; Bottom right:″ GL Archive/Alamy, 83: ″ Martin Heitner/Stock Connection/Aurora Photos, 85: ″ KRISTA ROSSOW/ National Geographic Creative, 92-93: © MICHAEL NICHOLS/ National Geographic Creative,102: © TAYLOR S. KENNEDY/ National Geographic Creative, 104: © KAZUHIRO NOGI/AFP/Getty Images,105: © StockLite/Shutterstock.com 107: © Andersen Ross/Getty Images; Left, 108: © Sarah2/Shutterstock.com; Top left: © Agnieszka Guzowska/ Shutterstock.com; Top right: © VR Photos/Shutterstock.com; Bottom left: © Ariel Schrotter/Shutterstock.com; Bottom right, 109: © Laborant/ Shutterstock.com; Top left: © PhotoObjects.net/ Thinkstock; Top right: © I Ching Chen/Flickr/Getty Images; Bottom left: © S.Dashkevych/ Shutterstock. com; Bottom right, 115 (t) Adam Pretty/Getty Images; 118 (tl) ZUMA Press, Inc./Alamy Stock Photo, (tr) Brian J. Skerry/National Geographic Creative, 121 David Doubilet/National Geographic Creative, 124 Joel Sartore, National Geographic Photo Ark/National Geographic Creative, 132 (b) © Peter Beck/Corbis/ Aurora Photos; 134 (t) © elwynn/Shutterstock.com; 136 (t) © Ira Block/National Geographic Creative; 137 (b) © Oote Boe 3/Alamy; 140 (b) © Jon Burbank/Alamy.

Scope and Sequence

Critical Thinking	Writing	Vocabulary Extension
Focus Personalizing Synthesizing, Reflecting, Guessing Meaning from Context	**Language for Writing** Using simple present tense (negative) Using adverbs of frequency **Writing Goal** Write about the risks you take.	**Word Link** *-ous* **Word Partners** Nouns/Adjectives + *size*

Building Vocabulary and Spelling	Original Student Writing
Words with the sound of **aw** in **straw**	Writing about one important event that happened in the past

Critical Thinking	Writing	Vocabulary Extension
Focus Analyzing a Sequence Synthesizing, Evaluating, Guessing Meaning from Context	**Language for Writing** Giving reasons Using present continuous tense **Writing Goal** Describe an animal that is in danger.	**Word Forms** Comparative adjectives **Word Partners** Verbs + *about*

Building Better Vocabulary	Original Student Writing
Word Associations Using Collocations Parts of Speech	Writing about an important person

Building Vocabulary and Spelling	Original Student Writing
Words with the sound of **u** in **school**	Writing about a job or hobby

TAKING A RISK

1

Two men take a break during a 19-day
climb in Yosemite National Park.

THINK AND DISCUSS

1 "Taking a risk" means doing something dangerous
or uncertain. What risks do you sometimes take?
2 What kinds of people take a lot of risks in their lives?

A Look at the information on these pages and answer the questions.

  1. What are the people in the photo doing?

  2. Who are more likely to take risks—men or women? Younger people or older people?

B Use the correct form of the words in blue to complete the definitions.

If you _____ something, you like doing it.

If something is _____, it is not safe.

Your _____ controls your body.

WHAT IS A RISK-TAKER?

Risk-takers know something bad can happen, but they don't worry about it. A skydiver—a person who jumps from an airplane as a sport—is an example of a risk-taker. It can be **dangerous** to jump from an airplane, of course. But a risk-taker **enjoys** this type of danger.

Psychologists—scientists who study the human **brain**—say that most risk-takers become bored easily. They enjoy the excitement of a risk. Who takes risks? Psychologists say men usually take more risks than women. And the greatest risk-takers are male teenagers.

Skydivers make a star formation above the clouds in Boituva, Brazil.

Reading 1 QUICK READ SEE PAGE 114

PREPARING TO READ

BUILDING
VOCABULARY
 A The words in **blue** below are used in the reading passage on pages 5–6. Match the correct form of each word with its definition.

Mountain climbing can be a dangerous **activity**, but it's also a very popular one. These days, more people than ever are climbing the world's highest peaks, thanks to the growing number of **businesses** that provide professional mountain guides. It's not just the **pleasant** views that people enjoy. What many people love is the experience of going through dangerous **situations**, often feeling **afraid**, but finally **succeeding** in achieving their **goal**.

1. _____ (n) a company that makes money by buying and selling things

2. _____ (n) something you want to achieve, or a reason for doing something

3. _____ (n) the conditions and events happening at a certain time and place

4. _____ (n) something that you spend time doing

5. _____ (adj) nice or enjoyable

6. _____ (adj) worrying that something bad will happen

7. _____ (v) to get the result that you were trying to achieve

USING
VOCABULARY
 B Note answers to the questions below. Then share your ideas with a partner.

1. Do you have a **goal** for learning English? What is it?

_____

2. When was the last time you felt **afraid**? Why did you feel this way?

_____

3. Would you like to try any dangerous **activities**? If yes, which ones?

_____

PREDICTING
 C Read the title and subheads of the reading passage on pages 5–6. What do you think the reading is mainly about? Check your answer as you read the passage.

a. the risks that professional skiers take
b. new research into risk-taking
c. different types of risk-takers

A ski jumper flies through the air during a tournament in Innsbruck, Austria.

LIVING ON THE EDGE

🎧 Track 1

A   Some people ski down mountains. Others climb huge rocks or photograph **dangerous** animals. Why do people **enjoy** risky **activities** like these?

THRILL SEEKERS

B   Some people take risks simply because it makes them feel good. Psychologist Marvin Zuckerman says that thrill seekers are always looking for change and excitement. When people do something new or risky, a chemical in the **brain** creates a **pleasant** feeling. Thrill seekers love this feeling and want to experience it as often as possible.

GOAL-DRIVEN RISK-TAKERS

C   Other people don't take risks for the thrill but to achieve a **goal**. For example, conservationist[1] Mike Fay went on a dangerous 2,000-mile expedition in central Africa. He worked to help save the wildlife there. Fay's expeditions helped create 13 national parks.

[1]A **conservationist** is someone who works to take care of the environment.

PROFESSIONAL RISK-TAKERS

D For other people, such as extreme athletes,[2] taking risks is part of their job. Sports psychologist Shane Murphy says extreme athletes see the world differently. In a dangerous activity such as skydiving, most people probably do not feel in control.[3] Extreme athletes are different: They feel in control in dangerous **situations**. The danger can even help them. For example, skier Daron Rahlves says that being **afraid** makes him try harder to **succeed**.

EVERYDAY RISK-TAKERS

E Most of us are not extreme athletes or explorers. However, we still take risks in our lives. Some of us take social risks, such as speaking in front of a large group of people, or talking to people we don't know at a party. Sometimes we take financial risks, such as buying a house. And sometimes we take career risks, such as leaving a job or starting a **business**. Most people take risks in some areas of life, but not in others. What kind of risk-taker are you?

[2]An **athlete** is someone who is very good at a sport or physical activity.
[3]If you are **in control** of something, you have power over it.

Trading on the stock market is a financial risk that many people take.

UNDERSTANDING THE READING

A Match the sentence parts to complete definitions of the four types of risk-takers.

UNDERSTANDING MAIN IDEAS

1. A thrill seeker _____
2. A goal-driven risk-taker _____
3. A professional risk-taker _____
4. An everyday risk-taker _____

a. takes many small risks in their daily life.
b. takes risks because it makes them feel good.
c. takes risks as part of their job.
d. takes risks to achieve an aim.

B Answer the questions. Circle the correct options.

UNDERSTANDING DETAILS

1. Why do people feel good when they take risks?
   a. because the brain releases a chemical
   b. because the heart works faster than usual

2. What was Mike Fay's goal?
   a. to help protect animals in Africa
   b. to help poor people in Africa

3. What does skier Daron Rahlves say about being afraid?
   a. He felt afraid at first but doesn't anymore.
   b. Being afraid helps him in his sport.

C Match the sentence parts to make true statements about the people mentioned in the passage.

IDENTIFYING EXAMPLES

1. Marvin Zuckerman _____
2. Mike Fay _____
3. Shane Murphy _____
4. Daron Rahlves _____

a. is an example of a goal-driven risk-taker.
b. is an example of a professional risk-taker.
c. believes some people take risks in order to feel good.
d. says extreme athletes cope better with danger than others.

> **CRITICAL THINKING** When you **personalize** something, you take a new idea and apply it to your own situation. It can help you understand and remember an idea better.

D Note answers to the questions below. Then discuss with a partner.

CRITICAL THINKING: PERSONALIZING

1. Think of a time when you took a risk. What type of risk was it: social, financial, career, or something else? Complete the sentence below.

   I took a _____ risk when I _____
   _____

2. Why did you take the risk? How did you feel afterwards?

   _____
   _____

DEVELOPING READING SKILLS

READING SKILL Guessing Meaning from Context

You can use the context—the words around the word—to guess the meaning of a new word. For example, the context might give the definition, an example, or an explanation that says the same thing with different words. The context can also help you decide the word's part of speech (e.g., noun, verb, adjective).

*Others climb **huge** rocks or photograph dangerous animals.*

The sentence above comes from the reading passage on pages 5–6. We know the passage is about risk, so we can guess that *huge* probably means "very big." We can also guess that the word is an adjective, as it appears before a noun and after a verb.

GUESSING
MEANING FROM
CONTEXT

 A Find and underline the following words in the reading on pages 5–6. Write the words next to the correct definitions. Then write the part of speech (e.g., noun, verb, adjective). Check your answers in a dictionary.

| **create** (Paragraph C) | **thrill** (Paragraph C) | **extreme** (Paragraph D) |
| **expedition** (Paragraph C) | **social** (Paragraph E) | **financial** (Paragraph E) |

1. _____ a trip with a special goal   part of speech: _____

2. _____ relating to groups of people   part of speech: _____

3. _____ relating to money   part of speech: _____

4. _____ a feeling of great excitement   part of speech: _____

5. _____ very far from the average   part of speech: _____

6. _____ to make something new   part of speech: _____

GUESSING
MEANING FROM
CONTEXT

B Read the paragraph below. Then match the words to the correct definitions. Check your answers in a dictionary.

Like many extreme athletes, Emily Cook was a risk-taker from a young age. "I was one of those kids," she says, "who enjoyed and **excelled** at anything **acrobatic**, anything where you were upside down." When she was older, Cook became the U.S. aerials ski champion—a sport where skiers perform acrobatics at great **heights**. "There are definitely moments," she explains, "when you're up there doing a new trick and it seems like the stupidest thing in the world. But **overcoming** that fear is just the coolest feeling."

_____ 1. **excel**   a. (n) a place far above the ground

_____ 2. **acrobatic**   b. (v) to be very good at

_____ 3. **height**   c. (adj) involving difficult physical acts

_____ 4. **overcome**   d. (v) to successfully deal with a problem

Video

Wildlife expert Brady Barr often works with dangerous animals like crocodiles.

KILLER CROCS

BEFORE VIEWING

A Look at the photo and read the caption. What is Brady Barr's job? Why is his job sometimes dangerous?

DISCUSSION

B The words in **bold** are used in the video. Match each word with the correct definition.

VOCABULARY IN CONTEXT

> People who hunt small animals often use **snares**.
>
> Bears and tigers can be **aggressive** if they are frightened.
>
> **Rangers** know a lot about animals and the environment.
>
> Chimpanzees can **rip** branches off trees and use them as tools.
>
> Conservationists often **rescue** animals that are in danger.

1. _____ (adj) wanting to fight

2. _____ (n) a person who takes care of a forest or a large park

3. _____ (v) to save from danger

4. _____ (v) to tear

5. _____ (n) a trap for catching animals

C Read the information. Complete the notes with your ideas. Then share with a partner.

Nile crocodiles are the largest reptiles on Earth. They live in rivers and swamps in Africa. These enormous animals can grow up to 6 meters in length, and can weigh up to 730 kg. They mainly eat fish, but will attack almost anything nearby, such as zebras, small hippos, birds, and even other crocodiles. They can eat up to half their body weight in one meal.

Nile crocodiles:

– can be about as long as ＿＿＿＿＿＿ humans lying end to end

– can weigh around ＿＿＿＿＿＿ times more than an average human male

– can eat about ＿＿＿＿＿＿ kg of food in one meal

WHILE VIEWING

A Watch the video. Answer the questions.

1. Why are the crocodiles in Uganda killing people?

   a. The crocodiles don't have enough food.

   b. People are attacking the crocodiles.

   c. People are feeding the crocodiles.

2. How is Brady Barr helping?

   a. He's catching the crocodiles so they can be trained not to attack humans.

   b. He's trying a new piece of technology used for catching crocodiles.

   c. He's teaching the local rangers to catch and move the crocodiles.

B Watch the video again. Number the steps from the video in the correct order (1–6)

____ a. close the crocodile's mouth

____ b. get close to the crocodile

____ c. take the crocodile to a new place

____ d. use the snare to pull the crocodile out

__1__ e. find the crocodile

____ f. sit on the crocodile's back

AFTER VIEWING

A Would you like to work with dangerous animals? Why or why not? Discuss with a partner.

B Think about the types of risk-takers you read about on pages 5–6. In your opinion, what kind of risk-taker is Brady Barr? Check (✓) more than one option if necessary. Discuss your answer with a partner.

☐ a thrill seeker   ☐ a professional risk-taker
☐ an everyday risk-taker   ☐ a goal-driven risk-taker

Reading 2   QUICK READ   SEE PAGE 117

PREPARING TO READ

A Read the sentences about climbing. The words in **blue** are used in the reading passage on pages 12–13. Match the correct form of each word with its definition.

BUILDING VOCABULARY

You need **strong** arms and legs to be a good climber.

Many successful rock climbers are **surprisingly** small in terms of their body **size**.

Free soloing is one of the riskiest forms of climbing. It involves climbing in high places **without** any ropes.

Bouldering is another type of climbing. Like free soloing, no ropes are used. But bouldering is safer because if you fall, you're usually quite **close** to the ground.

When climbing indoors, the **difficulty** of different routes is usually marked with different colors. Climbers **follow** the color that matches their ability. Following a route that's too difficult can get you into **trouble**.

1. _____ (n) problems

2. _____ (n) how easy or hard something is

3. _____ (n) how big or small something is

4. _____ (prep) not using or having

5. _____ (adv) used to describe something that wasn't expected

6. _____ (adj) near, not far

7. _____ (adj) having a lot of physical power

8. _____ (v) to move in the same direction as something in front of you

B List three ideas for each category below. Then share your ideas with a partner.

USING VOCABULARY

1. three sports in which you need to be **strong**

   _____   _____   _____

2. three countries that are **close** to your country

   _____   _____   _____

3. three animals that are about the **size** of a small car

   _____   _____   _____

C Read the title and look at the photos on pages 12–13. What do the two people in the passage do? What is risky about these activities? Discuss with a partner.

PREVIEWING

RISK-TAKERS

🎧 Track 2

A For some people, taking risks is part of their everyday lives. Here are two examples.

Ashima Shiraishi bouldering in Texas, U.S.A.

TEENAGE ROCK CLIMBER

B **Ashima Shiraishi** is still in high school, but she's one of the best climbers in the world. In rock climbing, climbers use ropes and other equipment to climb large rocks. In bouldering, participants climb rocks up to six meters high **without** any special equipment, so they have to be very **strong**.

C Bouldering has **difficulty** ratings from V0 to V16. In 2016, Shiraishi climbed a level V15 boulder called Horizon. She was only the second person to climb it. And at 14 years old, she was also the youngest person, and the first female climber.

D Shiraishi knows that the sport is dangerous—she once fell more than 10 meters while climbing indoors—but she continues to climb in the most difficult places around the world. Why does she do it? "My dream is to keep on pushing myself, and, maybe, I will push the sport itself," Shiraishi says. "I feel like if people are expecting me to do this, eventually, I will."

UNDERWATER PHOTOGRAPHER

E **Brian Skerry** is an underwater photojournalist. As part of his job, Skerry travels the world and goes diving with dangerous sea animals. To get the best photos, Skerry needs to get as close as possible—even if it's dangerous.

F While diving in New Zealand, Skerry found himself swimming next to a right whale. It was the size of a city bus. "Nobody is going to believe this," thought Skerry. "I've got to get this picture!" He swam fast so he didn't lose the whale, but he quickly became tired and had to stop. **Surprisingly**, the whale stopped as well. It waited for him and then began to follow him around. "It was like swimming around with a friend," Skerry says.

G Why does Skerry take these risks? He hopes his photographs will make people think about life in the world's oceans. "The oceans are in real trouble," he says. "As a journalist, the most important thing I can do is to bring awareness."

Brian Skerry's dive partner appears tiny next to a right whale.

UNDERSTANDING THE READING

UNDERSTANDING MAIN IDEAS

A Complete the diagram according to the information given in the reading passage.

a. takes part in risky activities
b. spends time with dangerous animals
c. travels around the world
d. once had a climbing accident
e. achieved something amazing at a young age
f. works to help the environment

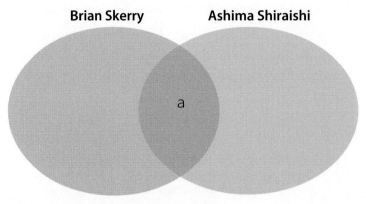

Brian Skerry   **Ashima Shiraishi**

a

UNDERSTANDING QUOTES

B Answer the questions. Circle the correct option.

1. What is Skerry referring to when he says, "It was like swimming around with a friend"?

   a. his relationship with his dive partner   b. the way a right whale followed him

2. What does Shiraishi mean when she says, "My dream is to keep on pushing myself"?

   a. She will keep trying to climb more difficult things.   b. She needs to become stronger to be successful.

CRITICAL THINKING: GUESSING MEANING FROM CONTEXT

C Find and underline the following words in the reading on pages 12–13. Write the words next to their definitions. Then write the part of speech (e.g., noun, verb, adjective). Check your answers in a dictionary.

> **awareness** (paragraph G)   **equipment** (paragraph B)   **participants** (paragraph B)

1. _____ things you need to do a particular activity   part of speech: _____

2. _____ knowing that something is there   part of speech: _____

3. _____ people who join an activity   part of speech: _____

CRITICAL THINKING: REFLECTING

D Think about the risk-takers in this unit. Which person takes the biggest risks? Why do you think so? Complete the sentence and then share your ideas with a partner.

I think …

☐ Daron Rahlves   ☐ Brian Skerry   ☐ Ashima Shiraishi   ☐ Brady Barr

takes the biggest risks because _____

_____

Writing

EXPLORING WRITTEN ENGLISH

A Read the information in the box.

> **LANGUAGE FOR WRITING** Simple Present Tense (Negative)
>
> We use the simple present for habits, daily routines, facts, or things that are generally true. We use the negative form of the simple present to say what is NOT true.
>
> To form the negative simple present with *be*, add *not* after *be*.
>
> *I'm a skydiver. I **am not** a skier. / I**'m** not a skier.*
> *Daron Rahlves is a skier. He **is not** a skydiver. / He**'s** not a skydiver.*
> *Skiing and skydiving are risky activities. Walking and dancing **are not** risky activities. / Walking and dancing **aren't** risky activities.*
>
> To form the negative simple present with other verbs, use *do + not + verb*.
>
> *I always travel with other people. I **do not** (or **don't**) **like** to travel alone.*
> *Daron Rahlves **does not** (or **doesn't**) **feel** afraid in dangerous situations.*
> *Barr and Skerry take professional risks. They **do not** (or **don't**) have easy jobs.*

Now complete each sentence (1–8) with the negative simple present form of the verb in parentheses.

Example: Risk-takers _____don't like_____ *(not like) to be bored.*

1. I _____ (*not enjoy*) going to parties alone.

2. Financial risk-takers _____ (*not be*) afraid to buy stocks.

3. Shiraishi _____ (*not use*) equipment when she climbs boulders.

4. Risk-takers _____ (*not be*) nervous in dangerous situations.

5. The crocodiles in Uganda _____ (*not have*) enough food.

6. My parents _____ (*not agree*) that I should quit my job.

7. Career risk-takers _____ (*not be*) afraid to leave their job.

8. I _____ (*not want*) to work in an office.

Skier Daron Rahlves competing in the Alpine Skiing World Cup

B Rewrite the following sentences (1–6). Change them to negative statements.

Example: *Barr avoids dangerous animals.*

Barr doesn't avoid dangerous animals.

1. Martin Zuckerman is an extreme athlete.

2. Most people enjoy dangerous activities.

3. Most of us are extreme athletes.

4. I take a lot of risks.

5. Brian Skerry works in the jungle.

6. The right whale is a small animal.

C Write five sentences in your notebook using the negative simple present. Write about things you DON'T do in order to stay healthy.

Example: *I don't take the subway to school every day. I sometimes walk.*

EDITING PRACTICE

Read the information. Then find and correct one mistake in each of the sentences (1–5).

In sentences with the negative simple present, remember to:

- include the correct form of *be:* *I* **am** *not;* *he / she / it* **is** *not;* *we / you / they* **are** *not.*
- use the correct form of *do:* *I / you / we / they* **do** *not;* *he / she / it* **does** *not.*
- use the base form of the verb after *do + not.* For example: *I don't* **like** *dangerous activities.*

1. I don't wanting to go skateboarding.
2. Most people does not like to take risks.
3. We not enjoy dangerous sports.
4. Brady Barr do not live in Uganda.
5. Good students do not to start studying for a test at the last minute.

D Read the information in the box.

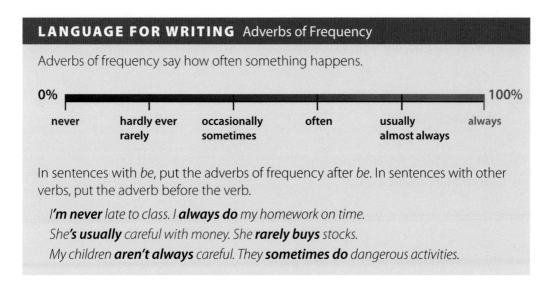

LANGUAGE FOR WRITING Adverbs of Frequency

Adverbs of frequency say how often something happens.

0% ——————————————————————————————————— 100%

never   hardly ever   occasionally   often   usually   always
         rarely   sometimes   almost always

In sentences with *be*, put the adverbs of frequency after *be*. In sentences with other verbs, put the adverb before the verb.

I'm never late to class. I always do my homework on time.
She's usually careful with money. She rarely buys stocks.
My children aren't always careful. They sometimes do dangerous activities.

Now put the adverbs of frequency in parentheses in the correct places in the sentences (1–6).

                occasionally
                   ᵛ
Example: Teenagers drive too fast. (occasionally)

1. It's safe to skateboard without a helmet. (*never*)

2. Skydivers wear protective suits. (*almost always*)

3. Skerry meets dangerous sea creatures in his work. (*often*)

4. Surfing is dangerous. (*sometimes*)

5. I take chances with my money. (*rarely*)

6. Shy people talk to strangers at parties. (*hardly ever*)

E How often do you do these activities (1–4)? Discuss your answers with a partner. Then write your answers using adverbs of frequency.

Example: A: Do you ever travel alone?
           B: No, I never travel alone. ⟶ I never travel alone.

1. travel alone: _____

2. speak in front of large groups: _____

3. talk to strangers at parties: _____

4. study for a test at the last minute: _____

WRITING TASK

GOAL You are going to write sentences on the following topic:
What risks do you take? What risks don't you take?

PLANNING   **A** Brainstorm answers to the questions below. Make notes in the chart. Don't write complete sentences.

What are some common risks that people take? Make a list.	
What kinds of risks do you take? Think of at least four examples.	
What kinds of risks do you never take? Think of at least four examples.	

FIRST DRAFT   **B** Use your notes above to write three sentences about risks you take and three sentences about risks you don't take. Use adverbs of frequency.

EDITING   **C** Now edit your draft. Correct mistakes with the negative simple present and adverbs of frequency. Use the checklist on page 130.

UNIT REVIEW

Answer the following questions.

1. What are two examples of an everyday risk?

_____

_____

2. Which of these is NOT an adverb of frequency?

  a. always   b. quickly   c. usually

3. Do you remember the meanings of these words? Check (✓) the ones you know. Look back at the unit and review the ones you don't know.

Reading 1:

☐ activity	☐ afraid	☐ brain
☐ business	☐ dangerous	☐ enjoy
☐ goal	☐ pleasant	☐ situation
☐ succeed		

Reading 2:

☐ close	☐ difficulty	☐ follow
☐ size	☐ strong	☐ surprisingly
☐ trouble	☐ without	

NOTES

Verbs: Simple Past Tense

An Indian bride and groom held hands on their wedding day.

OBJECTIVES **Grammar:** To learn about simple past tense
Vocabulary and Spelling: To study common words with the sound of <u>aw</u> in <u>straw</u>
Writing: To write about one important event that happened in the past

Can you write about one important event in the past?

Grammar for Writing

I **visited** the Vietnam Veterans Memorial Wall.

Simple Past Tense

✓ In **simple past tense**, regular verbs end in **–ed: need → needed**

✓ In simple past tense, irregular verbs change in different ways: **go → went**

✓ In simple past tense, each verb has only one form, so you use **needed** or **went** after all subjects.

✓ Three common time phrases for simple past tense include **yesterday, last _____,** and **_____ ago.**

    We **needed** more gas for our car **yesterday**, so we **went** to the gas station.

    I **did** my homework **last** night.

    She **arrived** here two weeks **ago**.

Regular Verbs in Simple Past Tense

Study this chart of regular verbs.

	want	**look**	**play**	**include**
Singular	I **wanted**	I **looked**	I **played**	I **included**
	you **wanted**	you **looked**	you **played**	you **included**
	he **wanted**	he **looked**	he **played**	he **included**
	she **wanted**	she **looked**	she **played**	she **included**
	it **wanted**	it **looked**	it **played**	it **included**
Plural	we **wanted**	we **looked**	we **played**	we **included**
	you **wanted**	you **looked**	you **played**	you **included**
	they **wanted**	they **looked**	they **played**	they **included**

✓ Most English verbs (99.9 percent) are regular verbs that add –ed for simple past tense:
   want → wanted

✓ For verbs that end in –e already, add only –d: **include → included**

✓ For verbs that end in consonant + y, change the –y to –i and add –ed: **try → tried**

✓ For verbs that end in vowel + y, add –ed: **enjoy → enjoyed**

✓ The –ed ending has three pronunciations, but the final spelling is always –ed: **needed** /əd/, **finished** /t/, and **played** /d/.

Single or Double Consonant?

One Syllable	
+ –ed	**double consonant + –ed**
wanted	stopped
needed	planned
added	robbed
looked	

Two Syllables	
+ –ed	**double consonant + –ed** (when the accent is on the second syllable)
happened	occurred
opened	permitted
followed	
returned	

✓ For one-syllable verbs that end in consonant + vowel + consonant (CVC), double the last letter before adding –ed.

✓ For two-syllable verbs that end in consonant + vowel + consonant (CVC), double the last letter before adding –ed only if the pronunciation stress is on the second syllable.

ACTIVITY 1 **Practicing the 30 Most Common Regular Past Tense Verbs in Writing***

Write the past tense of the 30 most common verbs in English writing.

present	past		present	past
1. want	_____		11. include	_____
2. ask	_____		12. receive	_____
3. start	_____		13. decide	_____
4. seem	_____		14. try	_____
5. use	_____		15. call	_____
6. show	_____		16. play	_____
7. report	_____		17. look	_____
8. turn	_____		18. appear	_____
9. die	_____		19. help	_____
10. work	_____		20. move	_____

*Source: Corpus of Contemporary American English and General Service List

	present	past		present	past
21.	happen	_____	26.	live	_____
22.	add	_____	27.	create	_____
23.	learn	_____	28.	believe	_____
24.	continue	_____	29.	suggest	_____
25.	open	_____	30.	like	_____

ACTIVITY 2 **Writing Sentences with Regular Past Tense Verbs**

Use one word from each of the four groups to write five new sentences. Be careful with capital letters, verb form (–ed), and periods. Follow the example.

Subject	Verb	Object	Time
he	watch	a football game	last night
we	play	a DVD	yesterday
they	enjoy	a basketball game	three days ago

Example: _We watched a DVD last night ._____

1. _____

2. _____

3. _____

4. _____

5. _____

ACTIVITY 3 **PAIR WORK: Who Has the Most Sentences That Are Different?**

Work with another student. Compare your sentences from Activity 2. You receive one point for each sentence that your partner does not have.

  1st time: _____ / 5 points possible

When you finish, work with another student. Each different sentence receives one point.

  2nd time: _____ / 5 points possible

  Your total: _____ / 10 points possible

Irregular Verbs in Simple Past Tense

Study this chart of irregular verbs in simple past tense.

	be	have	do	take	think
Singular	I **was** you **were** he **was** she **was** it **was**	I **had** you **had** he **had** she **had** it **had**	I **did** you **did** he **did** she **did** it **did**	I **took** you **took** he **took** she **took** it **took**	I **thought** you **thought** he **thought** she **thought** (Note: <u>It</u> is not usually used with **thought**.)
Plural	we **were** you **were** they **were**	we **had** you **had** they **had**	we **did** you **did** they **did**	we **took** you **took** they **took**	we **thought** you **thought** they **thought**

✓ English has thousands of verbs, but only a very small number of useful verbs—perhaps 150—are **irregular.**

✓ In English, these irregular verbs are used very often. In fact, the top ten verbs in English are all irregular: **was/were, had, did, said, came, got, went, made, took, thought.**

✓ Many verbs for daily activities are irregular: **eat ➔ ate; drink ➔ drank; speak ➔ spoke; wake ➔ woke.**

✓ For the verb **be**, you use **was** after **I, he, she, it**. Use **were** after **you, we,** and **they**. All other verbs have only one form for all subjects: **I went / she went / they went.**

ACTIVITY 4 **Practicing the 30 Most Common Irregular Past Tense Verbs in Writing***

Write the present tense of these irregular verbs that are in simple past tense.

present	past	present	past
1. _____	was	11. _____	thought
2. _____	were	12. _____	knew
3. _____	had	13. _____	told
4. _____	did	14. _____	saw
5. _____	said	15. _____	found
6. _____	came	16. _____	began
7. _____	got	17. _____	felt
8. _____	went	18. _____	became
9. _____	made	19. _____	gave
10. _____	took	20. _____	left

Source: Corpus of Contemporary American English

present	past	present	past
21. _____	wrote	26. _____	ran
22. _____	heard	27. _____	kept
23. _____	sat	28. _____	held
24. _____	stood	29. _____	brought
25. _____	put	30. _____	lost

ACTIVITY 5 **Writing Sentences with Irregular Past Tense Verbs**

Answer each question with a complete sentence. Pay attention to spelling, capital letters, and periods. Follow the example. When you finish, work with another student to compare answers.

Example: What time did you come to class today?

I came to class at 9 o'clock. _____

1. What time did you get up this morning?

_____

2. Where did you go last summer?

_____

3. When were you born?

_____

4. How much pasta did you eat last week?

_____

5. When did you do your homework?

_____

6. How many pets did you have ten years ago?

_____

7. Where did you buy your shoes?

_____

8. How many e-mails did you write last month?

_____

Common Student Mistakes

Student Mistake X	Problem	Correct Example ✓
<u>Mizumi an</u> e-mail to her parents.	verb missing	Mizumi **wrote** an e-mail to her parents.
We **live** in London in 2010.	past tense missing	We **lived** in London in 2010.
John and I **goed** to Brazil in 2005.	past tense form	John and I **went** to Brazil in 2005.
I **was** took Bus 87 yesterday.	extra verb	I **took** Bus 87 yesterday.

ACTIVITY 6 **Correcting Mistakes with Past Tense Verbs in Context**

Each sentence has a verb mistake. Correct the mistake. Then write each sentence again, but pay attention to capital letters, commas, and periods.

Some Strong Medicine

1. i catch a cold two or three days ago

   _____

2. last night i feel a little sick

   _____

3. i was took two aspirins and then i went to bed

_____

4. i usually got up at 8 o'clock but today i got up at 6:30

_____

5. i were very sick so i went to see my doctor

_____

6. he sayed i had a very high fever

_____

7. he was told me to go home and rest

_____

8. on the way home, i stopped at the drugstore

_____

9. i was buy some stronger medicine

_____

10. maybe i will felt better tomorrow

_____

Negative of Verbs in Simple Past Tense

Making a negative is very easy. You use the special helping verb **did** before the word **not**:
did not + verb. (The verb should be the simple or base form.)

✓ Use **did not** with all verbs (except **was, were, could, would**).

✓ With **was, were, could,** and **would,** just add **not** after the word.

✓ You can also use a short form (called a **contraction**) in speaking and in friendly writing such as
e-mail: **didn't.** Do not use contractions in formal writing.

	be	have	do	take
Singular	I **was <u>not</u>**	I **<u>did not</u> have**	I **<u>did not</u> do**	I **<u>did not</u> take**
	you **were <u>not</u>**	you **<u>did not</u> have**	you **<u>did not</u> do**	you **<u>did not</u> take**
	he **was <u>not</u>**	he **<u>did not</u> have**	he **<u>did not</u> do**	he **<u>did not</u> take**
	she **was <u>not</u>**	she **<u>did not</u> have**	she **<u>did not</u> do**	she **<u>did not</u> take**
	it **was <u>not</u>**	it **<u>did not</u> have**	it **<u>did not</u> do**	it **<u>did not</u> take**
Plural	we **were <u>not</u>**	we **<u>did not</u> have**	we **<u>did not</u> do**	we **<u>did not</u> take**
	you **were <u>not</u>**	you **<u>did not</u> have**	you **<u>did not</u> do**	you **<u>did not</u> take**
	they **were <u>not</u>**	they **<u>did not</u> have**	they **<u>did not</u> do**	they **<u>did not</u> take**

Common Student Mistakes

Student Mistake X	Problem	Correct Example ✓
Andrea **no lived** in Korea in 2011.	negative form	Andrea **did not live** in Korea in 2011.
We **do not arrived** late.	forms of helping verb and main verb	We **did not arrive** late.
I did not **took** the bus yesterday.	form of main verb	I did not **take** the bus yesterday.
Norah **was** not wake up at 7 this morning.	helping verb	Norah **did** not wake up at 7 this morning.

ACTIVITY 7 **Scrambled Sentences**

Change the order of the words to write a correct sentence. Be careful with spelling, capital letters, punctuation, and word order.

Omar's Difficult Final Test

1. english at omar college studies lincoln

   _____

2. reading yesterday final class the was for test his

   _____

3. difficult was test very the

_____

4. exam hours and was not two the took finish short, to it omar it

_____

5. short have did questions not the any test

_____

6. three the omar questions not to know did answers

_____

7. minutes his ago he a score out few found

_____

8. for good 81 a he score of that test, got difficult

_____

ACTIVITY 8 **Finding and Correcting 10 Mistakes**

Circle the ten mistakes. Then write the sentences correctly. The number in parentheses ( ) is the number of mistakes in that sentence. Be ready to explain your answers.

A Late Flight

1. My husband and I live in very small town in Texas. (1)

   _____

2. My mother come to visit us today, so we go to the airport to pick her up. (2)

   _____

3. Unfortunately, his flight did not arrived on time. (2)

   _____

4. The weather was very bad, almost all the flights tonight arrive late. (2)

   _____

5. My mother's flight was about two hour late. (1)

   _____

6. We finally were got home midnight before. (2)

   _____

Track 3 •)) **ACTIVITY 9** **Dictation**

You will hear six sentence three times. Listen carefully and write the six sentences. The number in parentheses ( ) is the number of words in the sentence. Be careful with capital letters and end punctuation.

1. _____ (8)

2. _____ (9)

3. _____ (8)

4. _____ (9)

5. _____ (6)

6. _____ (9)

ACTIVITY 10 **Practicing Grammar and Vocabulary in Model Writing**

Read the sentences in the paragraph very carefully. Fill in the missing words from the word bank. Circle the 19 letters that need to be capital letters. Then copy the paragraph on your own paper.

ingredients	covers	sauce	for	almost
daughter	pieces	juicy	in	food

A Special Event

1 my _____ laura loves italian food, and she knows how to cook very well.

2 she cooks a delicious italian chicken dish _____ every week. **3** she buys fresh

_____. **4** she cuts up onions, peppers, and garlic. **5** she fries them with some olive oil

_____ a large pan. **6** she cuts the chicken into small _____.

7 she puts a little flour on the chicken pieces. **8** she adds _____ to the fried vegetables.

9 she cooks everything for about ten minutes. **10** then she cuts up two large, _____

tomatoes and adds them to the pan. **11** laura also adds salt, pepper, and basil. **12** she does not add a lot.

13 she _____ the pan with a lid and lets everything cook _____

twenty minutes. **14** she tastes the _____ one last time to check the flavor.

15 a meal from laura is always a special event.

ACTIVITY 11 Guided Writing: Making Changes in Model Writing

Write the paragraph from Activity 10 again, but make your new sentences about yesterday's dinner. Make the changes listed below and all other necessary changes.

Sentence 2. Change **almost every week** to **yesterday.** Change the verb tense as necessary in all the sentences.

Sentences 4 and 5. Combine these two sentences with **and.**

Sentences 6, 7, and 8. Combine these three sentences with **and.** In sentence 7, use a pronoun for **chicken pieces.**

Sentences 11 and 12. Combine these two sentences with **but.**

Sentences 13, 14, and 15. Make sure you use the correct verb tense.

_____

_____

_____

_____

_____

_____

_____

_____

_____

_____

_____

_____

_____

Building Vocabulary and Spelling

Learning Words with the Sound of aw in straw *

aw = s t r **a w**   This sound is usually spelled with the letters **aw, au, all, al, ough,** and **ong**.

s t r a w

d r a w

ACTIVITY 12 **Which Words Do You Know?**

This list has 39 words with the sound of **aw** in str**aw**.

1. Notice the spelling patterns.

2. Check ✓ the words you know.

3. Look up new words in a dictionary. Write the meanings in your Vocabulary Notebook.

Common Words

GROUP 1:
Words spelled with **aw**

☐ 1. a w f u l
☐ 2. d r a w
☐ 3. d r a w e r
☐ 4. l a w
☐ 5. r a w
☐ 6. s a w
☐ 7. s t r a w

GROUP 2:
Words spelled with **au**

☐ 8. A u g u s t
☐ 9. a u t h o r
☐ 10. a u t o m o b i l e
☐ 11. a u t u m n
☐ 12. c a u g h t
☐ 13. c a u s e
☐ 14. d a u g h t e r

☐ 15. l a u n d r y
☐ 16. s a u c e
☐ 17. t a u g h t

GROUP 3:
Words spelled with **all**

☐ 18. a l l
☐ 19. b a l l
☐ 20. c a l l

*List is from: Spelling Vocabulary List ©2013 Keith Folse

☐ 21. f a l l

☐ 22. m a l l

☐ 23. s m a l l

☐ 24. t a l l

☐ 25. w a l l

GROUP 4:
Words spelled with **al**

☐ 26. a l m o s t

☐ 27. a l s o

☐ 28. a l w a y s

☐ 29. s a l t

☐ 30. t a l k

☐ 31. w a l k

GROUP 5:
Words spelled with **ough**

☐ 32. b o u g h t

☐ 33. b r o u g h t

☐ 34. c o u g h

☐ 35. t h o u g h t

GROUP 6:
Words spelled with **ong**

☐ 36. l o n g

☐ 37. s o n g

☐ 38. s t r o n g

☐ 39. w r o n g

ACTIVITY 13 **Matching Words and Pictures**

Use the list in Activity 12 to write the common word that matches the picture.

1. _____

3. _____

2. _____

4. _____

5. _____

7. _____

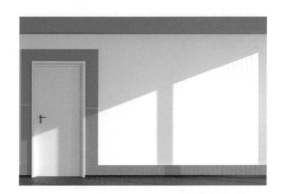

6. _____

8. _____

ACTIVITY 14 **Spelling Words with the Sound of <u>aw</u> in str<u>aw</u>**

Fill in the missing letters to spell words with the sound of **<u>aw</u>** in str<u>aw</u>. Then copy the correct word.

1. __ gust _____

6. __ ful _____

2. t __ ll _____

7. d __ ghter _____

3. r __ _____

8. __ lways _____

4. s __ ce _____

9. th __ ght _____

5. wr __ ng _____

10. dr __ _____

ACTIVITY 15 **Writing Sentences with Vocabulary in Context**

Complete each sentence with the correct word from Activity 14. Then copy the sentence with correct capital letters and punctuation.

1. maria used tomato ………… for her pasta dinner

_____

2. ling had only one ………… answer on the test so her score was 95

_____

3. my brother is very .... but my sister and I are short

_____

4. my sister .... about the problem for a long time

_____

5. we really like tennis so we .... play tennis on monday and thursday

_____

6. the month before september is ....

_____

7. this food is .... and I cannot finish it

_____

8. my wife and I have three sons and one ....

_____

9. it is very difficult to .... human hands

_____

10. sushi uses .... fish

_____

ACTIVITY 16 Scrambled Letters

Change the order of the letters to write a word that has the sound of **aw** in str**aw**.

_____	**1.** a t m n u u	_____	**8.** s t a l o m
_____	**2.** e s a u c	_____	**9.** w r a d
_____	**3.** w l a	_____	**10.** g l o n
_____	**4.** l a b l	_____	**11.** t t a g h u
_____	**5.** a l l f	_____	**12.** l a c l
_____	**6.** r o h t a u	_____	**13.** b g h r t u o
_____	**7.** s o a l	_____	**14.** k l a w

Track 4 ●)) ## ACTIVITY 17 Spelling Practice

Write the word that you hear. You will hear each word two times.

1. _____	6. _____	11. _____
2. _____	7. _____	12. _____
3. _____	8. _____	13. _____
4. _____	9. _____	14. _____
5. _____	10. _____	15. _____

ACTIVITY 18 Spelling Review: Which Word Is Correct?

This review covers the different ways of spelling the sound of <u>aw</u> in str<u>aw</u> in this unit. Read each pair of words. Circle the word that is spelled correctly.

	A	B		A	B
1.	bot	bought	11.	athor	author
2.	fall	foll	12.	almost	allmost
3.	small	smal	13.	straw	straugh
4.	all	al	14.	solt	salt
5.	allso	also	15.	daughter	doughter
6.	wraung	wrong	16.	strang	strong
7.	sauce	sos	17.	draw	drau
8.	cose	cause	18.	caugh	cough
9.	rau	raw	19.	towl	tall
10.	caught	cawght	20.	wak	walk

ACTIVITY 19 Spelling Review

Read the four words in each row. Underline the word that is spelled correctly.

	A	B	C	D
1.	cought	caught	caght	caughte
2.	allmost	allmst	almust	almost
3.	practese	practes	practice	proctice
4.	doughter	doghter	dawter	daughter
5.	schooll	school	shool	shooll
6.	sonetimes	sonetines	sommetimes	sometimes
7.	imbortant	important	imbortent	importent
8.	laundy	loundy	laundry	loundry
9.	study	stady	estudy	estady
10.	future	fuetur	futur	futoore
11.	cntinue	cantinue	continue	cuntinue

	A	B	C	D
12.	smoke	smok	esmoke	esmok
13.	jus	juis	juise	juice
14.	cusent	cousin	cousine	cusin
15.	amizeng	amizing	amazing	amazeng
16.	pic	pick	bic	bick
17.	aftar	eftar	after	aftair
18.	problem	proplem	problam	proplam
19.	trable	travle	trouble	trouvle
20.	little	littil	leetil	leetle
21.	reeson	reasone	raison	reason
22.	Wendsday	Wednesday	Windsday	Wednisday
23.	famous	famos	femos	faimous
24.	usully	usualli	usuali	usually
25.	Chainese	Chinese	Chineese	Chinees

Original Student Writing

Writing Your Ideas in Sentences or a Paragraph

Write six to twelve sentences on your own paper. Write about one important event that happened in the past. Examples include a birthday, a graduation, a very happy day, or a very important event to you. Use simple past tense verbs. For help, you can follow the examples in Activity 7, Activity 8, or Activity 11.

Peer Editing

Exchange papers from the above activity. Read your partner's sentences.
Then use Peer Editing Sheet 1 on ELTNGL.com/sites/els to make comments about the writing.

NOTES

SAVING THE WILD 3

An endangered sifaka—
a type of lemur

THINK AND DISCUSS

1 Which of the world's animals are disappearing? Why are they disappearing?
2 What can people do to help save animals in danger?

A Read the information below and answer the questions.

1. What human activities can be dangerous for animals?
2. Which animal in the photos is most in danger?
3. What kinds of information does the IUCN use to make its Red List?

B Use the correct form of the words in blue to complete the definitions.

If something is _____, there is a chance something bad will happen to it.

The _____ of something is how hot or cold it is.

If something has a(n) _____ on something else, it changes it.

ANIMALS IN DANGER

Animal species[1] in many parts of the world are **in danger** of becoming extinct.[2] In many cases, the greatest danger is humans. For example, human activity has an **effect** on temperatures around the world. As **temperatures** change, some animals find it difficult to survive. Humans also often build on land where animals live and find food. As a result, many animals lose their homes, or habitats.

The IUCN[3] Red List is a list of animal species that are in danger. The IUCN looks at how many of each animal live in the wild. It also looks at how the population is changing over time. The three highest levels of danger are **Vulnerable**, **Endangered**, and **Critically Endangered**.

[1] A **species** is a type of animal or plant.
[2] If an animal is **extinct**, there are no more left in the world.
[3] International Union for Conservation of Nature

VULNERABLE

Blue crowned pigeons are now only found on the island of New Guinea, in the South West Pacific. Hunting and habitat loss are the main dangers for these beautiful birds.

ENDANGERED

Chimpanzees live in Africa. Their population is falling fast, mainly because of habitat loss. Since the 1970s, the number of chimpanzees has fallen about 50 percent.

CRITICALLY ENDANGERED

There are only between 110 and 130 **blue-throated macaws** left in the forests of Bolivia.

Giant pandas are a small success story for conservation. In 2016, their status on the IUCN Red List changed from Endangered to Vulnerable.

Reading 1 QUICK READ SEE PAGE 120

PREPARING TO READ

BUILDING
VOCABULARY

A The words in **blue** below are used in the reading passage on pages 45–46. Which of these words are antonyms (words with opposite meanings)? Complete the sentences.

> Polar bear populations continue to **fall** because of climate change.
>
> Camels usually live in **warm** countries like Egypt and Saudi Arabia.
>
> As sea levels **rise**, many animals lose their habitats.
>
> There are just **over** 100 blue-throated macaws left in the wild.
>
> Global warming is most dangerous to animals that prefer **cool** temperatures.
>
> Some scientists believe black rhinos may become extinct in **under** 10 years.
>
> Birds build their nests high in the trees to keep their eggs **safe**.

1. _____ is the opposite of **in danger**.

2. _____ is the opposite of **fall**.

3. _____ is the opposite of **warm**.

4. _____ is the opposite of _____.

USING
VOCABULARY

B List three ideas for each category below. Then share your ideas with a partner.

1. three countries with a population of **under** 10 million

   _____   _____   _____

2. three animals that like to live in **cool** places

   _____   _____   _____

3. three things that are **rising** in your country

   _____   _____   _____

PREDICTING

C You are going to read about sea turtles and how their numbers around the world are falling. What might be causing this? Make a list of possible reasons. Check your predictions as you read the passage.

_____

_____

_____

SEA TURTLES FEEL THE HEAT

🎧 Track 5

A   Sea turtles are some of the oldest species in the world. The first sea turtles lived over 200 million years ago. Today, however, sea turtles are in danger. Their numbers are falling because of human activities and climate change.

B   Around the world, conservationists are studying the effects of climate change on sea turtles. They believe it affects them in a number of ways. First, sea levels are rising because of higher temperatures. As this happens, beach areas become flooded.[1] Sea turtles lay their eggs in the beach sand, so flooding can destroy[2] sea turtle nests and the eggs inside them.

C   Climate change has another effect on the turtles' eggs. In cooler temperatures, more male turtles are born. So, as the world becomes warmer, more female turtles are born than males. Scientists think that soon there may be no males at all.

[1]If a place is **flooded**, there is a lot of water covering land that is usually dry.
[2]If you **destroy** something, you damage it so badly that it dies or no longer works.

An endangered baby green sea turtle

Mariana Fuentes is a conservationist who works to protect sea turtles.

However, there are people who are trying to help. Conservationists such as Mariana Fuentes study the turtles and work hard to keep them safe. "To give marine turtles a better chance," she says, "we have to protect[3] their nesting sites."

D There are now projects in place at many turtle nesting sites around the world. These projects help to protect the turtle eggs from other animals and from humans. Sometimes eggs are also moved to cooler, safer areas.

There are some success stories, too. In the early 1990s, there were fewer than 5,000 green sea turtle nests in Florida. Because of conservation work, this number was up to just under 30,000 by 2015. But the turtles still have a lot of challenges, and Fuentes believes that they still need our help.

E "Turtles were here long before humans," she says. "It would be a complete tragedy[4] if they were to become extinct as a result of our actions."

[3]If you **protect** something, you try to keep it safe.
[4]A **tragedy** is a very sad event.

A female green sea turtle, Georgetown, Ascension Island

UNDERSTANDING THE READING

A Match a paragraph (A–E) from the reading with its main idea.

_____ 1. Many people around the world are helping to keep sea turtle eggs safe.

_____ 2. Warmer temperatures affect sea turtle eggs.

_____ 3. Sea turtles are an old species, but they are now in danger.

_____ 4. Sea turtle numbers are rising in some places, but the turtles still need our help.

_____ 5. Climate change is causing problems for sea turtles.

B Use the information in the passage to answer the questions. Circle the correct option.

1. Which of the following is NOT mentioned as a danger to sea turtles?

   a. climate change

   b. people stealing eggs

   c. trash in the ocean

2. What does Mariana Fuentes say we should do to help sea turtles?

   a. stop people from going to beaches where sea turtles lay eggs

   b. move more sea turtles to zoos

   c. keep sea turtle nests and eggs safe

3. Why is Florida mentioned in the passage?

   a. It is a place where conservation efforts are working.

   b. Mariana Fuentes studies sea turtles there.

   c. There are no more sea turtles there.

A baby sea turtle hatches from its egg.

> **CRITICAL THINKING**   A **sequence** is the order in which a series of events happen. To understand a sequence, it is often useful to make notes in the form of a flow chart.

C Find and underline information on pages 45–46 that describes two effects of climate change on sea turtles. Then complete the flow chart. Check your answers with a partner.

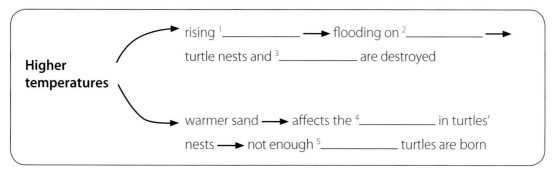

Higher temperatures

rising ¹_____ → flooding on ²_____ →
turtle nests and ³_____ are destroyed

warmer sand → affects the ⁴_____ in turtles' nests → not enough ⁵_____ turtles are born

DEVELOPING READING SKILLS

READING SKILL Identifying Reasons

Words such as *because* (*of*) and *since* introduce reasons.

*The number of chimpanzees is falling **because** their habitats are disappearing.*
       result   reason

***Because of** human activity, many animal habitats are disappearing.*
      reason   result

***Since** people are using more land for farming, many animals are losing their food sources.*
      reason   result

So introduces a result. It follows a reason.

*Climate change is melting Arctic ice, **so** the polar bears' habitat is disappearing.*
      reason   result

ANALYZING   **A**   Read the two paragraphs. Circle the words that introduce a reason or a result. Then answer the questions.

Giant pandas became endangered because people began to farm in their habitats. Farming destroyed the pandas' main food source. However, the Chinese government created areas for the pandas to live in, so now they have a better chance of surviving.

1. Why did giant pandas become endangered?

   _____

2. Why do they have a better chance of surviving now?

   _____

Some people kill sea turtles for food. However, since the ocean has dangerous chemicals in it, the turtles' bodies have these chemicals in them, too. People can get sick from eating turtles because of the chemicals in the meat.

1. Why can people get sick from eating sea turtles?

   _____

2. Why are sea turtles' bodies polluted?

   _____

APPLYING   **B**   Reread the following paragraphs in the reading on pages 45–46. Answer the questions. Then underline the information that gives you the answers.

Paragraph A: Why are sea turtle populations getting smaller?

   _____

Paragraph E: Why is the number of sea turtles in Florida increasing?

   _____

Video

A lemur at the Duke
Lemur Center, U.S.A.

SAVING LEMURS

BEFORE VIEWING

A Look at the photo on this page and the one on page 50. What do you know about these animals? How would you describe them? Discuss with a partner.

DISCUSSION

B Read the information about lemurs. Then discuss these questions.

LEARNING ABOUT
THE TOPIC

Lemurs are primates—like monkeys, gorillas, and humans. There are about 100 species, and they are all found on the island of Madagascar. Lemurs vary in shape and size, from the 9 kg indri lemur to the tiny mouse lemur. Some mouse lemurs weigh just 30 g and are only around 10 cm long. Sadly, lemurs are thought to be the world's most endangered primates. It is believed that 90 percent of all lemur species could become extinct in the next 20 to 25 years.

1. Did any of the information about lemurs surprise you?

   _____

2. Why do you think lemurs are endangered?

   _____

C The words and phrases below are used in the video. Match each word or phrase with the correct definition.

> If babies **gain weight**, they get bigger. This usually means they are healthy.
>
> To **take care of** baby animals, people keep them warm and give them food.
>
> Gorillas and chimpanzees are close **relatives**. They are both a type of ape.
>
> It's important to **make sure** that baby animals eat good food and are healthy.

1. _____ (v) to become heavier

2. _____ (v) to check that something is happening

3. _____ (v) to keep (someone or something) safe

4. _____ (n) members of the same family

WHILE VIEWING

A ▶ Watch the video. Which of the following are true about the Duke Lemur Center? Check (✓) all that apply.

☐ 1. It has the largest collection of lemurs outside Madagascar.

☐ 2. Only one person works there.

☐ 3. It takes care of lemur babies.

B ▶ Watch the video a second time and answer the questions.

1. Why is it an exciting time at the Duke Lemur Center?
   a. a new species of lemur has been found
   b. some lemur babies have been born

2. How can you check if lemur babies are healthy?
   a. by weighing them
   b. by looking at their eyes

3. What do the babies do during their first 30 days?
   a. learn to climb
   b. eat and sleep

A mouse lemur at the Duke Lemur Center

AFTER VIEWING

A What does Chris Smith mean when he says, "When you look into a lemur's eyes, you can tell that they're looking back"? Note your ideas below. Then discuss with a partner.

_____

B Which animal would you like to help more: lemurs or sea turtles? Why? Complete the sentence below with your own ideas, and then compare with a partner.

I would like to help _____ because _____

_____

Reading 2 QUICK READ SEE PAGE 123

PREPARING TO READ

A The words in **blue** below are used in the reading passage on pages 52–55. Match the correct form of each word to its definition. Circle the two words that are antonyms.

BUILDING VOCABULARY

Extinction has long been a part of **nature**. You might be **shocked** to learn that over 90 percent of the species that have ever lived on Earth are now extinct. Scientists think that in the last 600 million years, there have been five mass extinction events. Mass extinctions happen when many species **disappear** in a relatively short time. The last mass extinction happened 65 million years ago, and caused the extinction of the dinosaurs. The **latest** research suggests that, **unfortunately**, we may now be going through a sixth mass extinction—this time caused by human activities. **Fortunately**, many people **care about** animals and are working hard to **save** as many as possible.

1. _____ (n) everything in the world that is not made by people

2. _____ (adv) sadly or unluckily

3. _____ (v) to go away or become unable to be seen

4. _____ (v) to be interested in something and think it is important

5. _____ (v) to keep something away from danger

6. _____ (adj) the most recent

7. _____ (adj) very surprised or upset

8. _____ (adv) happily or luckily

B Note answers to the questions below. Then share your ideas with a partner.

USING VOCABULARY

1. Which animals do you **care about** the most? Why?

   _____

2. What animals do you know about that have **disappeared** forever?

   _____

C Look at the pictures and read the title and captions on pages 52–55. What is the reading mainly about? Check your idea as you read the passage.

PREDICTING

a. photographs of the world's most endangered animals
b. a photographer who takes pictures to help save endangered species
c. advice on how to take photographs of endangered animals

ANIMALS IN THE FRAME

🎧 Track 6

A   **Nature** photographer Joel Sartore uses his camera to **save** endangered species. Sartore's photos tell the stories of animals that may **disappear** unless we work fast to save them.

B   Sartore's **latest** project is called Photo Ark. You can see some photos from the project on pages 53–55. The goal of the project is to make a photographic record of as many animals as possible before they become extinct. As Sartore says, "For many of Earth's creatures, time is running out."[1]

Q   **How did you become interested in saving endangered species?**

A   When I was a child, I read about Martha, the very last passenger pigeon. Martha died in 1914. I was **shocked**. In the past, there were 5 billion passenger pigeons— probably more than any other bird. But here was the last one, and there was no way to save it. How did we let this happen? I couldn't understand it. I still feel the same way. I want to stop this from ever happening again.

Q   **How does photography help to save endangered species?**

D   **A**   Photography is the best way to show problems to the world. It gets people to **care about** the problems. It's not enough to just show pretty animals in beautiful places. Now we must show the dangers to these animals as well. The good news is there are many ways to publish[2] stories and photographs on environmental issues. Self-publishing on the Web is one way to do this. Even nonprofessional photographers can help to let people know about these problems.

---

[1]If you **run out** of something, you have no more of it left.
[2]When you **publish** information, you print it in a book or put it online.

◀ **Martha, believed to be the last passenger pigeon, died in 1914. Only 100 years earlier, these birds were found in large numbers throughout North America.**

▲ A bison poses for a Photo Ark photo. Sartore uses either white or black backgrounds for his photos.

Malayan tiger, Omaha Zoo

Malayan tigers are critically endangered. "We tried photographing him on a big black background," Sartore says, "but he just destroyed it. He looked like he really enjoyed it, too!" Fortunately for Sartore, the tiger didn't have a problem with white paper.

Madagascan fish eagle, Madagascar

Sartore took this beautiful photo at a zoo in Madagascar. Unfortunately, this eagle is one of the most endangered birds in the world. According to recent studies, the population in the wild is under 100.

The lemur leaf frog is another critically endangered animal. The species was once common in South America, but its population has fallen by 80 percent in the last 10 years. The main causes are disease and loss of habitat.

Lemur leaf frog,
Atlanta Botanical Gardens

Chimpanzee, Lowry Park Zoo

This three-month-old baby chimpanzee is called Ruben. "Ruben's mother left him," says Sartore, "so people at the zoo are raising him. While I took the photo, his caregivers were gently holding him. Baby primates are much like human children—they need a mother to hold on to, even if it's human."

UNDERSTANDING THE READING

UNDERSTANDING
MAIN IDEAS

A Complete the answers to the questions. Then underline the information in the passage that helped you.

1. Why was Sartore shocked when he read about Martha?

   Because _____.

2. Why does Sartore think that photography can help save endangered species?

   Because photography _____.

UNDERSTANDING
DETAILS

B Match each animal from the reading (1–5) with the correct information (a–e).

1. The passenger pigeon _____   a. is named "Ruben."
2. The Madagascan fish eagle _____   b. is extinct.
3. The lemur leaf frog _____   c. has fallen in number by 80 percent.
4. The chimpanzee _____   d. has a population of fewer than 100.
5. The tiger _____   e. tore up Sartore's black paper.

CRITICAL THINKING:
GUESSING MEANING
FROM CONTEXT

C Find and underline the following words in the reading. Use context to identify their meanings. Then complete the definitions.

creature (paragraph B)	**record** (paragraph B)	**issues** (paragraph D)

1. A(n) _____ is a collection of information.
2. A(n) _____ is an important subject or problem.
3. A(n) _____ is a living thing that is not a plant.

CRITICAL THINKING:
EVALUATING

D Note answers to the questions below. Then discuss with a partner.

1. How do the Duke Lemur Center and Joel Sartore help to save endangered species?

Duke Lemur Center	Joel Sartore

2. Which approach do you think is more useful in terms of saving animals?

   I think _____'s approach is more useful because

   _____

   _____

   _____

Writing

EXPLORING WRITTEN ENGLISH

A Read the information below.

LANGUAGE FOR WRITING Giving Reasons

You can use *because* to introduce a reason.

  Many animals are in danger **because** temperatures around the world are rising.
     result   **reason**

You can use *so* to introduce a result.

  Joel Sartore takes photos of endangered animals, **so** more people know about them.
       reason   **result**

Notice the comma in the sentence with *so*.

Now read the sentences (1–5). Label each sentence part *reason* or *result*.

1. Fuentes was interested in sea turtles, so she decided to help protect them.

   _____   _____

2. Australia is a good place to study sea turtles because it has a large turtle population.

   _____   _____

3. Fuentes works to protect sea turtles because human activity is endangering them.

   _____   _____

4. Sartore wanted to help endangered species, so he started his Photo Ark project.

   _____   _____

5. It's difficult to see Brazilian porcupines in the wild because they sleep during the day.

   _____   _____

**Joel Sartore carefully
photographs a caiman.**

B Complete the following sentences (1–5). Circle *because* or *so*.

1. The world population is increasing, **because** / **so** there are more cars on the road.
2. I want to help protect the environment, **because** / **so** I take the bus every day.
3. Some sea animals are dying **because** / **so** the ocean is polluted.
4. Sea turtles are critically endangered, **because** / **so** we need to help them.
5. Sartore created Photo Ark **because** / **so** he wanted to help save endangered species.

C Combine the sentences (1–5). Use the words in parentheses.

Example: I care about the environment. I ride a bicycle to work. (because)

I ride a bicycle to work because I care about the environment.

1. I take the bus to school every day. I want to save money. *(so)*

   _____

2. We recycle plastic. We don't want to pollute the oceans. *(because)*

   _____

3. We want to have cleaner air. Our city planted trees. *(because)*

   _____

4. I turn off the lights when I leave a room. I want to save electricity. *(so)*

   _____

5. We want to save trees. We use both sides of the paper. *(because)*

   _____

EDITING PRACTICE

In sentences with *because* and *so*, remember to:
- use *because* before a reason and *so* before a result.
- use a comma in sentences with *so*.

Find and correct one mistake in each of the sentences.

1. Some animals cannot cope with climate change so we need to help them.

2. Sartore publishes animal photos so he wants to help endangered species.

3. Fuentes wrote a book about sea turtles, so she wanted people to learn about them.

4. The number of male sea turtles is falling so climate change is affecting turtle eggs.

D Read the information below. Then complete the sentences with the present continuous form of the verb in parentheses.

LANGUAGE FOR WRITING Present Continuous Tense

We use the present continuous (*be* + verb-*ing*):

• to talk about actions happening now.

• to talk about situations that are changing.

*People around the world **are working** hard to save endangered animals.*

*The sea turtle population **is getting** smaller because people are **hunting** turtles.*

*Baby lemurs **are growing** and **getting** healthier in the Duke Lemur Center.*

---

1. Joel Sartore _____ (*make*) people more aware of endangered species with his photos.

2. The Duke Lemur Center _____ (*help*) to raise baby lemurs.

3. Lemurs are endangered because people _____ (*destroy*) forest habitats.

4. Polar bears _____ (*lose*) their habitats because the polar ice _____ (*melt*).

5. The Florida panther is a critically endangered species. However, conservationists _____ (*work*) hard to protect its forest habitats.

EDITING PRACTICE

In sentences with the present continuous tense, remember to:
• use *be* before an -*ing* verb.
• use the correct form of *be*.
• use an -*ing* verb after *be*.

Correct one mistake in each of the sentences.

1. In some places, sea turtle populations is going up.

2. Sea turtle habitats are in danger because temperatures rising.

3. Mariana Fuentes is help to protect sea turtles.

4. Humans is destroying many animals' habitats.

**A critically endangered ▶
Florida panther**

WRITING TASK

GOAL You are going to write sentences on the following topic:

Describe an animal that is in danger. Why is it in danger? What are people doing to help?

PLANNING **A** Choose an endangered animal from this unit that you are interested in. Then make notes about it below.

1. Endangered animal: _____

2. Where does this animal live? _____

3. How many are left in the world? _____

4. Why is it endangered? _____

5. What are people doing to help? _____

FIRST DRAFT **B** Use your notes to write at least five sentences about the animal. Use *because* or *so* and the present continuous tense.

_____

_____

_____

_____

_____

EDITING **C** Now edit your draft. Correct mistakes with *because*, *so*, and the present continuous tense. Use the checklist on page 129.

UNIT REVIEW
Answer the following questions.

1. What two words can you use to introduce a reason?

_____

_____

2. What is one result of climate change?

_____

_____

3. Do you remember the meanings of these words? Check (✔) the ones you know. Look back at the unit and review the ones you don't know.

Reading 1:

☐ cool   ☐ effect   ☐ fall

☐ in danger   ☐ over   ☐ rise

☐ safe   ☐ temperature   ☐ under

☐ warm

Reading 2:

☐ care about   ☐ disappear   ☐ fortunately

☐ latest   ☐ nature   ☐ save

☐ shocked   ☐ unfortunately

NOTES

People decided to paint their homes
bright colors in Itilleq, Greenland.

OBJECTIVES To learn the simple past tense of *be* and regular verbs
To learn the simple past tense of irregular verbs
To study the negative form of the simple past tense
To practice compound sentences with *but*
To study complex sentences to show time

Can you write about the home you lived in as a child?

Grammar for Writing See pages 130-140 for *What Is a Paragraph?*

The Simple Past Tense of *Be*

What happened yesterday? What happened 10 years ago? When we talk about actions in the past, we use the **simple past tense**. Both regular verbs and irregular verbs can be used in the simple past tense.

The most common verb in English, *be*, is an **irregular** verb.

Be	
I **was**	we **were**
you **were**	you (plural) **were**
he / she / it **was**	they **were**
✗ I am in Guatemala last year.	
✗ I were in Guatemala last year.	
✓ I was in Guatemala last year.	

The Simple Past Tense of Regular Verbs

Add *-ed* or *-d* to the end of **regular** verbs to form the simple past tense.

Visit	
I **visited**	we **visited**
you **visited**	you (plural) **visited**
he / she / it **visited**	they **visited**
Live	
I **lived**	we **lived**
you **lived**	you (plural) **lived**
he / she / it **lived**	they **lived**
✗ We call our parents yesterday.	
✓ We called our parents yesterday.	

There is more information on the spelling of regular simple past tense verbs on page 138 in the *Brief Writer's Handbook*.

Circle the regular simple past tense verbs. Then answer the questions using complete sentences.

Example Paragraph 1

A Great Leader

Cesar Chavez was an important **civil rights** leader in the United States. Chavez was born in Arizona to a Mexican-American family. Life was hard for his family there, so they moved to California. In California, most of the family needed to work in the fields picking lettuce. Working in the fields was difficult. His family received very little money, and people often treated them badly. Chavez stopped school in the eighth grade and started to work in the fields, too. Chavez wanted to make changes to field workers' lives. He was angry about the **discrimination** he saw. In the 1970s and 1980s, he organized many **boycotts** and **protests** against companies to **demand** better treatment for the workers. Like Gandhi and Martin Luther King, Jr., Chavez's protests were nonviolent. He often used **hunger strikes** to bring attention to his fight. Over time, thousands of people joined his peaceful cause. It was not always easy, but in his lifetime, Chavez helped to improve the lives of America's field workers.

civil rights: the legal rights that every citizen in a country has

discrimination: unfair treatment of a person because he/she belongs to a particular group

a boycott: a refusal to buy or use something as a protest

a protest: an act done to show strong disagreement about something

to demand: to strongly ask for something, especially if you feel it is your right

a hunger strike: when a person does not eat food for a long time to protest something

Post-Reading

1. Who was Cesar Chavez?

   _____

2. Where was he born?

   _____

3. What work did his family do?

   _____

4. What did he do when he stopped school in the eighth grade?

   _____

5. How did he fight against discrimination?

   _____

ACTIVITY 2 **Writing Sentences with the Simple Past Tense**

Rewrite the sentences. Change the verbs from the simple present to the simple past tense.

1. Julia Silverman and Jessica Matthews study at Harvard University.

   Julia Silverman and Jessica Matthews studied at Harvard University.

2. In class, an engineering professor asks them to solve a world problem.

_____

3. The women are not engineers, but they are creative.

_____

4. Julia and Jessica decide to create a playful energy source for the world.

_____

5. They study different countries with few power sources.

_____

6. In these countries, both adults and children play soccer daily.

_____

7. Julia and Jessica finally discover their idea!

_____

8. The women create a soccer ball with a battery inside.

_____

9. Jessica, Julia, and their friends work on many versions of the soccer ball.

_____

10. Finally, they develop a working ball!

_____

11. They decide to call the ball the SOCCKET.

_____

12. When someone kicks the SOCCKET, it captures the energy from the ball's motion.

_____

13. Then the battery stores the energy and powers LED lights and cell phones.

_____

14. Julia and Jessica introduce their product in El Salvador, Mexico, and South Africa.

_____

15. People use the SOCCKET and love it.

_____

ACTIVITY 3 Editing: Plural to Singular

Circle all of the simple past tense verbs. Then follow the directions, and make changes to the paragraph.

Example Paragraph 2

The Top of the Class

In 2008, Antonio Salazar and Marcus Quaglio (were) the top students at the University of North Carolina. They studied in the history department. They **excelled** in their studies. In class, they answered all of their instructors' questions. Their test scores were better than the other students', and their class projects received excellent marks. When they graduated in 2012, they finished at the top of the class. All of the teachers were very proud of Antonio and Marcus.

to excel: to do something very, very well

Now rewrite the paragraph on the lines on page 69 with these changes:

1. Change the male students' names to *Fatima Al-Otaibi*. (NOTE: *Fatima* is a woman's name.)

2. Change any pronouns or possessive adjectives to go with *Fatima*.

3. Change any other words necessary (such as *students* to *student* in the first sentence).

The Top of the Class

In 2008, Fatima Al-Otaibi was the top student at the University of North Carolina.

_____

_____

_____

_____

_____

_____

_____

_____

_____

_____

ACTIVITY 4 **Writing about an Important Person**

Think of an important person who lived in the past, such as a famous politician, singer, artist, or athlete. It could be a member of your family or a friend. (However, this person should not be alive.) Answer the questions using complete sentences.

1. Who was this person?

   _____

2. Where was the person born?

   _____

3. What was the person's job?

   _____

4. Why is the person important to you? What did he or she do?

   _____

   _____

   _____

5. How do you feel when you think about this person? Why?

   _____

   _____

Grammar for Writing

The Simple Past Tense of Irregular Verbs

Many verbs in English have an **irregular** past tense form. Here are some common irregular verbs.

Base Form	Simple Past	Base Form	Simple Past	Base Form	Simple Past
be	was/were	go	went	say	said
become	became	have	had	see	saw
buy	bought	leave	left	send	sent
do	did	make	made	sit	sat
eat	ate	pay	paid	speak	spoke
feel	felt	ride	rode	teach	taught
get	got	run	ran	write	wrote

✗ Last night, I <u>buy</u> a new CD.
✗ Last night, I <u>buyed</u> a new CD.
✓ Last night, I bought a new CD.

There is no special rule that tells when a verb is irregular. You must memorize the simple past tense. A dictionary will tell you when a verb is irregular.

There is a longer list of common irregular simple past tense verbs on page 139 in the *Brief Writer's Handbook*.

ACTIVITY 5 Practicing Irregular Verbs in the Past Tense

Circle the 13 irregular simple past tense verbs. Then answer the questions using complete sentences.

Example Paragraph 4

Helen Keller (1880–1968)

Helen Keller was a famous American author. Until Keller was two years old, she was a healthy and happy child. However, when she was two years old, she became very ill with an extremely high **fever**. The fever made her **deaf** and **blind**. Because she could not communicate with anyone, she became a wild and uneducated child. When she was seven years old, her parents hired Annie Sullivan to teach Helen. After many long struggles, Sullivan taught Helen to communicate with sign language. This **achievement** opened a new world to Keller. When Helen was 20 years old, she began taking college courses. After her graduation, she wrote 13 books and traveled around the world to talk about her life. She was an incredible human being.

a fever: a high temperature in the body

deaf: not able to hear

blind: not able to see

an achievement: something important that you are able to complete on your own

Post-Reading

1. Why was Keller blind and deaf?

_____

2. What happened when she became blind and deaf?

_____

3. What did Annie Sullivan do for Helen?

_____

4. What happened when Helen was 20 years old?

_____

5. What did Helen do after she graduated?

_____

Grammar for Writing

Time Phrases with the Simple Past Tense

Time phrases help to show that something happened in the past. Some of these time phrases include:

last night   last week   this morning   yesterday   (two minutes) ago

You can put these time phrases at the beginning or the end of a sentence. Avoid using them in the middle of a sentence.

✗ I yesterday scratched my knee.

✗ I scratched yesterday my knee.

✓ Yesterday I scratched my knee.

✓ I scratched my knee yesterday.

ACTIVITY 6 **Using Irregular Simple Past Tense Verbs**

Ask your partner the questions. Write each answer as a complete sentence. Use the irregular form of the simple past tense.

1. Where were you last summer?

   _____

2. How did you feel yesterday?

   _____

3. Where did you go last weekend?

   _____

4. When did you last see a funny movie?

   _____

5. What did you buy last week?

   _____

6. Who did you speak with yesterday?

   _____

7. When did you leave for school this morning?

   _____

8. When did you do your homework?

_____

9. Where did you eat lunch yesterday?

_____

10. When did you last send an e-mail?

_____

Grammar for Writing

The Simple Past Tense of *Be*: Negatives

Add the word *not* to make a negative sentence with *be*.

Subject	Be + Not	Subject	Be + Not
I	was **not**	we	were **not**
you	were **not**	you (plural)	were **not**
he / she / it	was **not**	they	were **not**

✗ I <u>did</u> not <u>be</u> at work last night.
✓ I was not at work last night.

Writer's Note

Contractions with the Negative Form of *Be*

Some contractions are possible with the verb *be* in negative form.

was not = wasn't   were not = weren't

Careful! Be sure that the apostrophe (') is placed directly before the letter *t*. Remember that the apostrophe takes the place of the missing *o* in *not*.

✗ She <u>is'nt</u> my sister.

✗ She <u>isn,t</u> my sister.

✓ She isn't my sister. (OR She's not my sister.)

✗ I <u>was'nt</u> in class yesterday.

✗ I <u>wasn,t</u> in class yesterday.

✓ I wasn't in class yesterday.

It is important to remember that contractions might be too informal for academic writing. Ask your instructor if using contractions in this course is acceptable.

Write the correct form of *be* in each blank. Be sure to use the negative form where indicated.

Example Paragraph 5

Moving to the United States

My name is Panadda, and I **1** _____

born in Thailand. I (**2** negative) _____ the first

child. My sister Suntri **3** _____ born three years

before I **4** _____ born. My parents (**5** negative)

_____ rich, but they **6** _____ always

happy. They **7** _____ hard workers. In 2012, we moved

to the United States. Everyone in my family **8** _____

very excited. We **9** _____ also scared. My mother

10 (negative) _____ able to speak English at all. When

we arrived, she began English classes. My sister and I started school.

We **11** (negative) _____ comfortable in the classroom

because we did not know the language. After a few years, however, we

learned the language and the culture of the United States.

Read the paragraph about Panadda's family in Activity 7 again. Think about your own family. Write a short paragraph about your family. Choose a time in the past, and use the simple past tense. Include at least one compound sentence in your paragraph.

_____

_____

_____

_____

_____

_____

_____

_____

_____

_____

_____

_____

_____

_____

Grammar for Writing

The Simple Past Tense: Negatives

Aside from the verb *be*, the negative form of all other verbs in the simple past is formed in the same way.

Subject	Did + Not	Base Form
I, you, he / she / it, we, you (plural), they	**did not**	**live** **visit** **do**

NOTE: Contraction: *did not = didn't*

✗ Ahmed <u>no finish</u> his homework.

✗ Ahmed <u>no finished</u> his homework.

✓ Ahmed did not finish his homework.

✗ Ella <u>no wrote</u> a report for her boss.

✗ Ella <u>did not wrote</u> a report for her boss.

✓ Ella did not write a report for her boss.

Unscramble the words to make correct sentences. Change the verbs to the negative simple past tense form.

1. live / in Johannesburg in 2010 / Carmen

   Carmen did not live in Johannesburg in 2010.
   _____

2. Ling / engineering / last semester / study

   _____

3. last year / him / Humberto's parents / visit

   _____

4. large brains / have / dinosaurs

   _____

5. me / help / Juan / with my homework

   _____

6. Emma / the letter / send / this morning / to her parents

   _____

7. with his academic advisor / speak / Karl / yesterday

   _____

8. I / my homework / yesterday / do

   _____

9. the party early / Janiel and Yosemy / last night / leave

   _____

10. go / my brother / last Saturday / to the grocery store

   _____

ACTIVITY 10 Editing: Writing Negative Simple Past Sentences

The sentences below are false. With a partner, rewrite each sentence using the negative form of the verb to make the sentence true. Then write a correct affirmative sentence. Follow the example.
NOTE: Some verbs are regular, and some are irregular.

There is a longer list of common irregular verbs on page 139 in the *Brief Writer's Handbook.*

1. John F. Kennedy was a leader in Mexico.

   John F. Kennedy was not a leader in Mexico. He was a leader in the United States.

2. Confucius lived in Colombia.

   _____

3. Zinedine Zidane played professional basketball.

   _____

4. Lady Gaga sang her songs in Arabic.

   _____

5. The *Titanic* sank in the Pacific Ocean.

   _____

6. Leonardo da Vinci came from Germany.

   _____

7. Albert Einstein invented the radio.

   _____

8. Stephen King wrote *Romeo and Juliet*.

   _____

ACTIVITY 11 **Reviewing the Simple Past Tense**

Fill in the blanks with the simple past tense of the verbs in parentheses. Write the negative form where indicated.

Example Paragraph 6

Bob's Horrible Day

Bob (**1.** have) _____ a horrible day on Monday.
First, he (**2.** be) _____ supposed to get up at 6 A.M.,
but his alarm clock (**3.** work, negative) _____ . He
(**4.** get up) _____ at 8 A.M. There (**5.** be, negative)
_____ any hot water for a shower, so he had to use cold
water. After that, his car (**6.** start, negative) _____ ,
and he had to take the bus. When Bob (**7.** get) _____
to work, his boss (**8.** yell) _____ at him for being
late. Next, his computer (**9.** crash) _____ , and he
(**10.** lose) _____ all of his documents. He (**11.** stay)
_____ at work until midnight to redo the documents. Bob
(**12.** decide) _____ to stay home the next day because he
(**13.** be) _____ too tired from all his bad luck.

Grammar for Writing

Using *But* Correctly

The connector *but* shows a contrast or difference between the ideas it connects.

Two simple sentences	I bought a car. John bought a truck.
One compound sentence	I bought a car, **but** John bought a truck.

But is not always a connector. Sometimes it is a preposition that means *except*. When *but* is used as a preposition, do not use a comma.

Compound Sentence (Use Comma)		Simple Sentence (No Comma)
We visited all the countries in South America, but we did not visit Chile.	=	We visited all of the countries in South America **but** (except) Chile.
All of the new cars are hybrid cards, but this one is not a hybrid car.	=	All of the new cars **but** (except) this one are hybrid cars.

ACTIVITY 12 **Using *But* as a Preposition**

Combine the two simple sentences into one simple sentence using *but* as a preposition (= *except*).

1. I ate all the food on my plate. I did not eat the spinach.

   _____

2. Every student in the class is wearing running shoes. Stephanie is not wearing running shoes.

   _____

3. The teacher asked everyone a question. The teacher did not ask Ryan and Joe a question.

   _____

4. My mother cleaned every room in the house. My mother did not clean my room.

   _____

5. The official language of every country in South America is Spanish. Spanish is not the official language of Brazil, Suriname, and French Guyana.

   _____

Reviewing Compound Sentences

Identify each sentence as a simple (*S*) or compound (*C*) sentence. If the sentence is compound, insert a comma where it is necessary.

1. ___*S*___ The girls practiced every day.

2. ___*S*___ They did not win the tennis tournament.

3. ___*C*___ The girls practiced every day, but they did not win the tennis tournament.

4. _____ The committee members made a decision but the manager did not like it.

5. _____ Neal worked with his father at the shoe store for almost twenty years.

6. _____ We went to Canada but we did not visit Toronto.

7. _____ With the recent increase in crime in that area of the city, the local residents there are worried about their safety.

8. _____ Summer is a good time to practice outdoor sports but winter is not.

9. _____ All of the workers but Marian arrived at yesterday's meeting on time.

10. _____ Saudi Arabia and Kuwait import equipment, cars, food, and medicine.

11. _____ The chairs in the living room are made of wood but the chairs in my office are made of metal.

12. _____ All of the chairs in the kitchen but this one are made of wood.

ACTIVITY 14 **Writing Compound Sentences**

Read each incorrect statement about two brothers. Then write a compound sentence with *but* that contains correct information. Use the information from the charts.

Name:	Andrew Bright
Born:	January 14, 1938
Died:	March 23, 2008
Home City:	Washington, DC
Education:	high school diploma
Work:	firefighter
Family:	wife and five children
Hobbies:	singing

Name:	Ian Bright
Born:	May 1, 1930
Died:	September 22, 2003
Home City:	Chicago, Illinois
Education:	college degree
Work:	high school math teacher
Family:	single
Hobbies:	playing baseball

1. They were born on the same day.

   Andrew was born on January 14, but Ian was born on May 1.

2. The brothers were born in the same year.

   _____

3. They both sang as a hobby.

   _____

4. Both brothers were married.

   _____

5. They lived in the same city.

   _____

6. They had the same level of education.

   _____

7. Both men had the same kind of job.

   _____

8. They died on the same date.

   _____

ACTIVITY 15 Interviewing Your Classmates

Ask different classmates the following questions. Write down their answers. Then use information about yourself and your classmates' answers to write compound sentences with *but*.

1. Where are you from? *Classmate's answer:* ___Peru_____

   I am from Kuwait, but José is from Peru.

2. What did you eat for dinner last night? *Classmate's answer:* _____

   _____

3. Where was your last vacation? *Classmate's answer:* _____

   _____

4. Why did you come to this school? *Classmate's answer:* _____

   _____

5. What country do you want to visit? *Classmate's answer:* _____

   _____

Grammar for Writing

Sentence Variety: Complex Sentences

When you write, sentence variety is important. This will make your writing more interesting. Good writers use both **simple** and **compound sentences**. There is another way to add variety to your sentence writing: **complex sentences**.

A complex sentence is a combination of two clauses. A **clause** is a group of words that includes a subject and a verb. In a complex sentence, one clause begins with a connecting word such as *after*, *before*, *when*, *until* and *as soon as*. The other clause has no connecting word.

Simple Sentences	Clause (subject + verb)	Clause (subject + verb)	
	John played tennis.	Vicky watched TV.	

Compound Sentence	Clause (subject + verb)	Connector	Clause (subject + verb)
	Joe played tennis,	and	Vicky watched TV.

Complex Sentence	Clause (subject + verb)	Clause (connector + subject + verb)	
	Joe played tennis	after Vicky watched TV.	

Compound sentences and complex sentences both use a connector to combine two clauses. However, the connector in a compound sentence is <u>not</u> part of the clauses. In a complex sentence, the connector is part of one clause.

In a complex sentence, the clause with the connector cannot be a sentence by itself. It is a fragment and must be connected to another sentence.

✗ <u>Until he bought a car.</u> (fragment) John rode his bicycle to work.

✓ Until he bought a car, John rode his bicycle to work.

✗ My mom made dinner. When my dad got home. (fragment)

✓ My mom made dinner when my dad got home.

Commas in Complex Sentences

When a complex sentence begins with a clause that contains a connecting word, put a comma at the end of the clause. Do not use a comma when the connecting word is in the middle of the sentence.

✗ After she ate dinner she called her friend.

✓ After she ate dinner, she called her friend.

✗ She called her friend, after she ate dinner.

✓ She called her friend after she ate dinner.

Identify each sentence as a simple (*S*), compound (*CD*), or complex (*CX*) sentence. If the sentence is compound or complex, insert a comma where it is necessary.

1. ____**S**____ Alexi and Juan finished their essays last night.

2. ___**CD**___ Karl saw a movie this weekend, but he thought it was really boring.

3. ___**CX**___ Before Mahmood left class, he spoke to the teacher about his homework.

4. _____ Amy expected to take a test today but she was wrong.

5. _____ The students did not have any questions after the teacher gave the assignment.

6. _____ My friends and I went down to the cafeteria and had lunch.

7. _____ We arrived at school early enough to get a coffee before class.

8. _____ We can study here or we can go to the library.

9. _____ I got a horrible grade on my first test but a good one this time.

10. _____ When Karen wanted information for her report she went to the library.

11. _____ We cannot take a break until we finish the project.

12. _____ Everyone but Ricky came to the study group.

13. _____ Sam began to study as soon as he got to the library.

14. _____ Ying decided to ask a friend to edit her paper and she liked her friend's comments.

Grammar for Writing

Using Complex Sentences to Show Time Order

You can use time words to show order in a sentence, for example *first, next, after that*. You can also use complex sentences with connectors such as *after* and *as soon as* to show time order. This will help add sentence variety to your writing.

After	Use this connector with the action that happened first.
With Time Words	First, Leila finished school for the day. Then she drove to work.
Complex Sentence	**After** Leila finished school for the day, she drove to work. OR Leila drove to work **after** she finished school for the day.

When	Use this connector with the action that happened first.
With Time Words	First, my sister got sick. Then the doctor gave her some medicine.
Complex Sentence	**When** my sister got sick, the doctor gave her some medicine. OR The doctor gave my sister some medicine **when** she got sick.

Before	Use this connector with the action that happened second.
With Time Words	First, Josh practiced driving. Next, he took the driver's license exam.
Complex Sentence	**Before** Josh took the driver's license exam, he practiced driving. OR Josh practiced driving **before** he took the driver's license exam.

As soon as	Use this connector with the first action when the second action happened very soon after the first action.
With Time Words	First, I arrived in Portland. Right after that, I toured the city.
Complex Sentence	**As soon as** I arrived in Portland, I toured the city. OR I toured the city **as soon as** I arrived in Portland.

NOTE: When the clause with the connector comes at the beginning of the sentence, you must use a comma after it.

ACTIVITY 17 Writing Complex Sentences in the Past

Combine the two simple sentences into a complex sentence. Use the connector in parentheses.

1. (as soon as)
   First: I graduated from high school.
   Second: I got a summer job.

   As soon as I graduated from high school, I got a summer job.

2. (before)
   First: Jack traveled around the world.
   Second: Jack began his English classes.

3. (when)
First: My sister and I finished our homework.
Second: My sister and I went to a movie.

_____

4. (after)
First: The house caught on fire.
Second: The fire department arrived very quickly to put out the fire.

_____

5. (before)
First: The young woman looked left and right.
Second: The young woman crossed the street.

_____

6. (when)
First: The lights in the classroom went out.
Second: The teacher told the students not to worry.

_____

7. (as soon as)
First: Jacob had the freedom to study abroad.
Second: Jacob moved to California to study English.

_____

Correct the paragraph. There are 15 mistakes. (If you need help finding the mistakes, look at the numbers in parentheses. These numbers tell you how many mistakes are in each line.) The first mistake has been corrected for you.

Example Paragraph 7

Muhammad Ibn Batuta

(3)   Ibn Batuta was a famous moroccan traveler. He live in Morocco

(1)   in the fourteenth century. When he was a man young, he made a

(1)   religious trip to Mecca. However, Ibn Batuta loves to see new places

(2)   so much that he continued to travel. This was no his original plan

(1)   but he continued on his journey. He had many adventures during her

(2)   travels and he met many interesting people. After he returned home

(2)   he did not forgot about his journey. He wrote a book about his travels,

(2)   this book now gives us a lot of information important about life in

(1)   the fourteenth century. Also, gives us more information about this

(1)   interesting and important man

Building Better Vocabulary

ACTIVITY 19   **Word Associations**

Circle the word or phrase that is most closely related to the word or phrase on the left. If necessary, use a dictionary to check the meaning of words you do not know.

	A	B
1. horrible	very bad news	very good news
2. a century	one hundred years	ten years
3. to communicate	to keep information	to share information
4. excellent	the best	the worst

5. to continue	to not stop	to pause
6. proud	a grade of 45 percent	a grade of 100 percent
7. to discriminate	negative action	positive action
8. to demand	to make a strong request	to make a weak request
9. to worry	to be excited	to be unhappy
10. to graduate	to complete school	to do little by little
11. the beginning	the first minute	the last minute
12. a manager	a boss	a teacher
13. original	a copy	not a copy
14. to arrive	to come to a place	to leave a place
15. to scare	to laugh	to scream

ACTIVITY 20 **Using Collocations**

Fill in each blank with the word that most naturally completes the phrase on the right. If necessary, use a dictionary to check the meaning of words you do not know.

1. before / first   the _____ thing to do

2. to / for   a trip _____ Puerto Rico

3. to / at   to arrive _____ the supermarket

4. information / communication   to share _____ about the problem

5. about / for   to have a question _____ your
            homework

6. against / on   to discriminate _____ someone

7. make / take   to _____ a decision

8. communication / vegetables   effective _____

9. freedom / beginning   the _____ to do anything
            that you want to do

10. afraid / excited   to be _____ about a new class

Study the word forms. Fill in each blank with the best word form provided. Use the correct form of the verb. If necessary, use a dictionary to check the meaning of words you do not know. (NOTE: The word in bold is the original word that appears in the unit.)

Noun	Verb	Adjective	Sentence Practice
pride	Ø	**proud**	1. She was very _____ when she graduated.
			2. I have a lot of _____ in my children.
excellence	**excel**	**excellent**	3. Damon _____ in swimming when he was younger.
			4. That was an _____ movie!
communication	**communicate**	communicative	5. We _____ by phone for three hours yesterday.
			6. Roberto was shy, but now he is more _____.
continuation	**continue**	continuous/ continual	7. The students _____ to study after the semester ended.
			8. The _____ traffic noise gave me a headache.
culture	Ø	cultural	9. I know about Indian _____.
			10. Kim and Jo's _____ differences are small.

Noun endings: *-ence, -ion, -tion*

Adjective endings: *-ent, -ive, -ous, -al*

Original Student Writing

ACTIVITY 22 **Original Writing Practice**

Reread the paragraph about Cesar Chavez on page 65 and your answers to Activity 4 on page 69. Then think of an important person (different from the person in Activity 4) that you want to write about.

Follow the steps to write a paragraph about this person. Use the simple past tense. Put a check (✓) next to each step as you complete it. When you finish your paragraph, use the checklist that follows to edit your work.

_____ STEP 1: In your first sentence, tell the name of the person and how that person was important.

_____ STEP 2: In your next sentence, write where the person was born.

_____ STEP 3: In the next sentence, tell about the person's job.

_____ STEP 4: In the next three or four sentences, tell a short story about the person. The story should show why the person is important.

_____ STEP 5: Make one compound sentence.

_____ STEP 6: Make one complex sentence.

_____ STEP 7: Use a negative verb in one of the sentences.

_____ STEP 8: In the last sentence, write why you chose this person.

_____ STEP 9: Use at least two of the vocabulary words or phrases presented in Activity 19, Activity 20, and Activity 21. Underline these words and phrases in your paragraph.

If you need ideas for words and phrases, see the Useful Vocabulary for Better Writing on pages 153–155.

☑ Checklist

1. ❑ I checked that each sentence has a subject and a verb.

2. ❑ I used the correct form of all the simple past tense verbs.

3. ❑ I began every sentence with a capital letter.

4. ❑ I capitalized all proper nouns (names, cities, countries, etc.).

5. ❑ I used commas correctly in compound and complex sentences.

6. ❑ I ended every sentence with the correct punctuation.

7. ❑ I gave my paragraph a title.

ACTIVITY 23 Peer Editing

Exchange papers from Activity 22 with a partner. Read your partner's paragraph. Then use Peer Editing Sheet 2 on ELTNGL.com/sites/els to help you comment on your partner's paragraph. Be sure to offer positive suggestions and comments that will help your partner improve his or her writing. Consider your partner's comments as you revise your own paragraph.

Additional Topics for Writing

Here are ten ideas for journal writing. Choose one or more of them to write about. Follow your teacher's directions. (We recommend that you skip a line after each line that you write. This gives your teacher a place to write comments.)

PHOTO
TOPIC: Look at the photo on pages 62–63. Describe a home you lived in when you were a child. How big was the house? What color was the house? Where was the house? What did you like or dislike about the house? What was your favorite room in the house?

TOPIC 2: Describe a vacation you took. Where did you go? What did you do? Who went on this vacation with you? How old were you when you went on this trip? Did you like this vacation?

TOPIC 3: Write about a movie you saw or a book you read. Did you like it? Who was your favorite character? What was the story about? Did the author have a message for the audience of this book or movie?

TOPIC 4: Write about what you did last weekend. Where did you go? Who did you go with? Did you enjoy it? Why or why not?

TOPIC 5: Write about a person you used to know. Who was this person? Where did you meet this person? What was special about this person?

TOPIC 6: Write about an important event in your life. How old were you? What happened? Why is this event important to you?

TOPIC 7: Describe a holiday that you and your family spent together. What was the occasion? Which family members were there? What did you do?

TOPIC 8: Write about something embarrassing that happened to you. How old were you? What happened? Why were you embarrassed? Who saw this happen? How did you feel afterwards?

TOPIC 9: Write about a day you spent outdoors. What did you do? Where did you go? Who did you go with? What specific activities did you do? How was the weather?

TOPIC 10: Describe a pet you had in the past. What was the pet's name? What kind of animal was it? How long did you have this pet? Why did you like (or dislike) this pet?

Timed Writing

How quickly can you write in English? There are many times when you must write quickly, such as on a test. It is important to feel comfortable during those times. Timed-writing practice can make you feel better about writing quickly in English.

1. Take out a piece of paper.

2. Read the writing prompt below.

3. Brainstorm ideas for five minutes.

4. Write eight to ten sentences.

5. You have 20 minutes to write.

Describe a sad (or happy, frightening, funny, important, etc.) event or time from your past. What was the event or time? Give examples of how this event or time made you feel that emotion.

_____

_____

_____

_____

_____

_____

_____

_____

_____

_____

_____

_____

_____

_____

Elephant orphans and their caregivers form great friendships in Nairobi National Park, Kenya.

Grammar: To learn about coordinating conjunctions **<u>and</u>**, **<u>but</u>**, **<u>so</u>**
Vocabulary and Spelling: To study common words with the sound of **<u>u</u>** in sch**<u>oo</u>**l
Writing: To write about a job or hobby

*Can you write about
someone's job or hobby?*

Grammar for Writing

I choose the two pairs of blue shoes, **but** *you can choose a different pair.*

Coordinating Conjunctions: <u>and</u>, <u>but</u>, <u>so</u>

✓ The **conjunctions and, but, so** can connect two clauses. (A clause has one subject-verb combination.)

✓ The words **and, but, so** are very common conjunctions. They are called **coordinating conjunctions** because they connect two equal parts to make a compound sentence.

Using <u>and</u> in Your Writing

✓ The word **and** is used when you want to give extra information.

✓ You use a comma before **and** when there are two clauses in the sentence.

✓ You do not use a comma with **and** when there are only two nouns, two verbs, or two adjectives.

✓ Do not write a sentence that begins with **and**.

Commas with <u>and</u>		
Example	**Explanation**	
Peru is in South America, **and** it has many high mountains.	Peru is …, **and** it has …	comma between two clauses: subject + verb, **and** subject + verb
Peru is in South America **and** has many high mountains.	Peru is … **and** has …	no comma: subject + verb **and** verb
Peru **and** Ecuador are in South America.	Peru **and** Ecuador	no comma: noun **and** noun (2 items in a list)
Peru, Ecuador, **and** Brazil are in South America.	Peru, Ecuador, **and** Brazil	commas with 3 items in a list: noun, noun, **and** noun

ACTIVITY 1 Using Commas with *and*

Add a comma in the box if it is necessary. On the line, write YES or NO and explain why you need or do not need a comma.

1. My name has five letters [,] and your name also has five letters.   YES – 2 clauses

2. Our favorite teachers are Mr. Foley [] and Mr. Wilson.   NO – 2 nouns

3. Apple pie is very sweet [] and it is my favorite dessert.   _____

4. China is a big country [] and it has many people.   _____

5. China is a big country [] and has many people.   _____

6. Becky [] and Sue are classmates [] and they live on the same street.   _____

7. The colors of the American flag are red [] white [] and blue.   _____

8. My first name has five letters [] and my last name also has five letters.   _____

9. Ten people work in my office [] and four of them are from Alaska.   _____

10. I like basketball very much [] and play it almost every weekend.   _____

11. I like basketball very much [] and I play it almost every weekend.   _____

12. Our favorite food is fish [] and we eat it three times a week.   _____

ACTIVITY 2 Writing Compound Sentences with *and*

Combine the two sentences to make a compound sentence with **and**. Use pronouns to avoid repeating a noun. Be sure to use a comma between the two clauses.

1. India is a large country. India has many people.

   India is a large country, and it has many people.

2. You add a little milk to your coffee. Then you drink your coffee.

   _____

3. That book has two hundred pages. That book costs twenty-two dollars.

   _____

4. Karen is from the United States. She lives in Michigan.

   _____

5. Bob and Sue are married. Bob and Sue have three children.

   _____

6. Minnesota is next to Canada. Minnesota has many lakes.

_____

7. A cheeseburger is delicious. A cheeseburger does not cost much.

_____

8. A giraffe has four long legs. A giraffe can run really fast.

_____

Using <u>but</u> in Your Writing

✓ The word **but** is used when you want to give different or opposite information.

✓ You use a comma before **but** when there are two clauses in the sentence.

✓ You do not use a comma with **but** when there is only one clause in the sentence.

✓ Do not write a sentence that begins with **but.**

Commas with <u>but</u>		
Examples	**Explanations**	
Frankfurt is a large city**, but** it is not the capital of Germany.	Frankfurt is … **, but** it is not …	comma between two clauses: subject + verb**, but** subject + verb
The weather in January is sunny **but** cold.	sunny **but** cold	no comma if there is one clause: adjective **but** adjective

ACTIVITY 3 **Writing Compound Sentences with <u>but</u>**

Combine the two sentences with **but**. Be sure to use a comma between the two clauses.

1. English has 26 letters. Arabic has 28 letters.

   English has 26 letters, but Arabic has 28 letters.

2. I love cheese. My brother loves vegetables.

   _____

3. Marcos is from Mexico. Claudio is from Argentina.

   _____

4. Shanghai is the largest city in China. Beijing is the capital.

   _____

5. July has 31 days. June has 30 days.

   _____

6. Wei is from China. Cho Hee is from Korea.

_____

7. Bolivia does not have a seacoast. Chile has a very long one.

_____

8. The number **two** is even. The number **nine** is odd.

_____

Using <u>so</u> in Your Writing

✓ The word **so** as a connector has two different meanings.

✓ Meaning 1: **My parents have brown eyes, so I have brown eyes.**
As a coordinating conjunction, **so** means "and the result is" or "therefore." In this case, you use a comma before **so**.

✓ Meaning 2: **I need better English so I can get a good job in the future.**
When **so** means "in order to" or "the purpose is," you do not use a comma. With this meaning, **so** is not a coordinating conjunction.

✓ Do not write a sentence that begins with **so** as a connector.

Commas with <u>so</u>		
Examples	**Explanations**	
My parents have brown eyes, **so** I have brown eyes.	My parents have … , **so** I have …	Meaning 1. Use a comma. (**so** means "the result is" or "therefore")
I need better English **so** I can get a good job in the future.	I need … **so** I can …	Meaning 2. Do not use a comma. (**so** means "in order to" or "the purpose is")

ACTIVITY 4 **Writing Compound Sentences with <u>so</u> (Meaning 1)**

Combine the two sentences with **so**. Use pronouns to avoid repeating a noun. Use a comma between the two clauses.

1. Luke has a car. Luke does not take a bus to school.

Luke has a car, so he does not take a bus to school.

_____

2. Each shirt is $50. Two shirts are $100.

_____

_____

3. I am a vegetarian. I do not eat hot dogs.

_____

_____

4. It will rain later today. You need an umbrella.

_____

_____

5. My computer is broken. I can not check my e-mail.

_____

_____

6. The weather in Florida is very hot in July. That is not a good time to visit the state.

_____

_____

7. The weather in Toronto in January is cold. You need a heavy coat.

_____

_____

8. That soup has pork. I can not eat that soup.

_____

_____

9. The word **on** has more than 20 meanings. The word **on** is difficult to learn well.

_____

_____

10. My sister runs five miles every day. My sister is in good shape.

_____

_____

ACTIVITY 5 **Writing Compound Sentences with <u>so</u> (Meaning 2)**

Combine the two sentences with **so**. Use pronouns to avoid repeating a noun. Do not use a comma between the two clauses.

1. Students wake up early. Students can get to class on time.

   Students wake up early so they can get to class on time.
   _____

2. Please study tonight. You will do well on tomorrow's test.

   _____

   _____

3. My mom adds a lot of onions to the rice. The rice will taste better.

   _____

   _____

4. You need to wear a coat. You will not be cold.

   _____

   _____

5. The best students ask questions. The best students can understand everything well.

   _____

   _____

6. I always use a pencil in math class. I can change my answers easily.

   _____

   _____

Common Student Mistakes

Student Mistake X	Problem	Correct Example ✓
Five is an odd **number but** six is an even number.	comma missing	Five is an odd number**,** but six is an even number.
I like tea, **<u>so</u>** I hate coffee.	wrong connector	I like tea, **but** I hate coffee. Or: I like tea, **and** I hate coffee.
Costa Rica is in Central America. **And** Peru is in South America.	beginning a sentence with a connector	Costa Rica is in Central America**,** **and** Peru is in South America.

ACTIVITY 6 **Unscrambling Clauses to Make Compound Sentences with** <u>and</u>, <u>but</u>, <u>so</u>

You will see two groups of words and a conjunction. Change the order of the words to write a correct English sentence with the conjunction. Be careful with capital letters, commas, and end punctuation.

1. A. cook a mother very my is good

   B. not make can pizza she

   conjunction: **but**

   My mother is a very good cook , but she can not make pizza .
   _____

   _____

2. A. my are from cousins France

   B. French speak they

   conjunction: **so**

   _____

   _____

3. A. swim day my every friends

   B. they good swimmers are very

   conjunction: **so**

   _____

   _____

4. A. much we India very like

   B. we plan to go there next month

   conjunction: **and**

   _____

   _____

5. A. math books table are the on the

   B. books are on the the science desk

   conjunction: **and**

   _____

   _____

6. A. Michael on vacation and Rob are

   B. one is at no their house

   conjunction: **so**

   _____

   _____

7. A. my easy math class is

   B. are difficult my classes English and Arabic

   conjunction: **but**

   _____

   _____

8. A. light breakfast my father eats a

   B. lunch he salad for eats

   conjunction: **and**

   _____

   _____

ACTIVITY 7 Scrambled Sentences

Change the order of the words to write a correct sentence. Be careful with spelling, capital letters, punctuation, and word order. (Hint: Five sentences need commas.)

Visiting the Zoo

1. children so to go to the zoo they love love animals

   _____

2. the animals zoo kinds has many different of

   _____

3. some really big animals are but small others are

   _____

4. elephants and are big animals giraffes camels

   _____

5. monkeys are animals small and penguins

   _____

6. my they are favorite like leopards so animal at the zoo i

_____

7. beautiful leopards really fast are can run and they

_____

8. and sister likes gazelles my pandas

_____

ACTIVITY 8 **Scrambled Sentences with <u>and</u>, <u>but</u>, <u>so</u>**

Change the order of the words to write a correct English sentence. Sometimes more than one answer is possible. Be careful with capital letters, punctuation, and word order.

1. small big libya panama is is a a but country country
   Panama is a small country, but Libya is a big country.

_____

_____

2. but wei faisal are and and amani ming china from dubai are from

_____

_____

3. my with so i will mr at 8:45 meeting currier is 9 at o'clock arrive

_____

_____

4. is the brazil not city sao paolo is the largest capital but it in

_____

_____

5. she likes it a new car very Elena has and much

_____

_____

6. canada not have a is but does large large a very country it population

_____

_____

7. thai read this speaks message help you phatra so she can

_____

_____

8. but a it is fruit sweet not a tomato is

_____

_____

ACTIVITY 9 **Finding and Correcting 10 Mistakes**

Circle the ten mistakes. Then write the sentences correctly. The number in parentheses ( ) is the number of mistakes in that sentence. Be ready to explain your answers.

Children's Day in Japan

1. Children's Day is a holiday very special in Japan. (1)

_____

2. People in Japan celebrate Children's Day on fifth day of fifth month, the date is easy to remember. (3)

_____

3. On this day, you can to see many colorful cloth fish flying in the air. (1)

_____

4. When the wind blow, the fish seem to be swimming in very fast river. (2)

_____

5. If these fish are strong, they will reach their home and they can be happy, and successful. (2)

_____

6. On this day Japanese parents hope their children will be strong like these fish. (1)

_____

Track 7 •)) **ACTIVITY 10** **Dictation**

You will hear six sentences three times. Listen carefully and write the six sentences. The number in parentheses ( ) is the number of words. Be careful with capital letters and end punctuation.

1. _____ (9)

2. _____ (11)

3. _____ (10)

4. _____ (11)

5. _____ (8)

6. _____ (10)

Practicing Grammar and Vocabulary in Model Writing

Read the sentences in the paragraph very carefully. Fill in the missing words from the word bank. Circle the 12 letters that need to be capital letters. Then copy the paragraph on your own paper.

walks	break	information	at	finishes	future
works	blocks	excellent	a lot	trips	company

My Brother John

1 this _____ is about my brother john. **2** john has an _____ job.

3 john likes it _____ . **4** john _____ in the travel office of

a large _____ . **5** his job is to plan _____ for people. **6** john lives

only four _____ from his office. **7** he _____ to work every day.

8 he starts work _____ 9 a.m. **9** he _____ work at 5 p.m.

10 he takes a _____ for lunch from 12:30 to 1:15. **11** i hope to have a great job like this

in the _____ .

ACTIVITY 12 | Guided Writing: Making Changes in Model Writing

Write the paragraph from Activity 11 again, but make the changes listed below and all other necessary changes.

Sentence 1. Change **brother** to **cousin.**

Sentence 2 and 3. Combine these two sentences with **and.**

Sentence 6. Change **only** to **just.**

Sentences 6 and 7. Combine these two sentences with **so.**

Sentences 8 and 9. Combine these two sentences with **and.**

Sentence 10. Add the adjective **short** in the correct place.

Sentence 11. Change **in the future** to **one day.**

_____

_____

_____

_____

_____

_____

_____

_____

_____

_____

_____

_____

_____

_____

Building Vocabulary and Spelling

Learning Words with the Sound of u in school *

$\underline{u}$ = s c h $\underline{oo}$ l   This sound is usually spelled with the letters **oo, ue, u +** consonant + final **e, ew, ou, o, ui, u,** and others.

school

blue

ACTIVITY 13   Which Words Do You Know?

This list has 42 common words with the sound of **u** in sch**oo**l.

1. Notice the spelling patterns.

2. Check ✔ the words you know.

3. Look up new words in a dictionary. Write the meanings in your Vocabulary Notebook.

Common Words

GROUP 1:
Words spelled with **oo**

☐ 1. c h o o s e

☐ 2. c o o l

☐ 3. f o o d

☐ 4. n o o n

☐ 5. p o o l

☐ 6. p o o r

☐ 7. r o o m

☐ 8. s c h o o l

☐ 9. s o o n

☐ 10. s p o o n

☐ 11. t o o

☐ 12. t o o t h

☐ 13. z o o

GROUP 2:
Words spelled with **ue**

☐ 14. b l u e

☐ 15. t r u e

☐ 16. T u e s d a y

GROUP 3:
Words spelled with **u** + consonant + final **e**

☐ 17. i n c l u d e

☐ 18. J u n e

☐ 19. r u l e

GROUP 4:
Words spelled with **ew**

☐ 20. f e w

☐ 21. k n e w

*List is from: Spelling Vocabulary List © 2013 Keith Folse

☐ 22. n e w

☐ 23. n e w s

☐ 24. n e w s p a p e r

GROUP 5:
Words spelled with **ou**

☐ 25. g r o u p

☐ 26. s o u p

☐ 27. y o u

GROUP 6:
Words spelled with **o** (at the end of the word)

☐ 28. d o

☐ 29. t o

☐ 30. t w o

☐ 31. w h o

GROUP 7:
Words spelled with **ui**

☐ 32. f r u i t

☐ 33. j u i c e

☐ 34. s u i t c a s e

GROUP 8:
Words spelled with **u** and pronounced **yu**

☐ 35. c o m p u t e r

☐ 36. c o n f u s e d

☐ 37. u s e

☐ 38. m u s i c

GROUP 9:
Other spellings

☐ 39. s h o e

☐ 40. s t u d e n t

☐ 41. w h o's

☐ 42. w h o s e

ACTIVITY 14 **Matching Words and Pictures**

Use the list in Activity 13 to write the common word that matches the picture.

1. _____

3. _____

2. _____

4. _____

5. _____

7. _____

6. _____

8. _____

ACTIVITY 15 **Spelling Words with the Sound of <u>u</u> in sch<u>oo</u>l**

Fill in the missing letters to spell words with the sound of <u>u</u> in sch<u>oo</u>l. Then copy the correct word.

1. wh __ _____

7. incl __ d __ _____

2. r __ l __ _____

8. T __ sday _____

3. kn __ _____

9. n __ _____

4. f __ _____

10. n __ s _____

5. t __ _____

11. n __ n _____

6. gr __ p _____

12. tr __ _____

Writing Sentences with Vocabulary in Context

Complete each sentence with the correct words from Activity 15. Then copy the sentence with correct capital letters, commas, and end punctuation.

1. the day after monday is …………

_____

2. ………… is the teacher for that ………… of students

_____

3. does your school have a ………… about coming to class on time

_____

4. there are a ………… books on the table but they are not …………

_____

5. a bill in a restaurant does not usually ………… a tip

_____

6. jonathan can speak chinese and he can write it …………

_____

7. sara ………… all the answers on the test yesterday so her score was 100

_____

8. the opposite of false is …………

_____

9. did you hear the international ………… program at ………… yesterday

_____

Scrambled Letters

Change the order of the letters to write a word that has the sound of **u** in sch**oo**l.

_____	1. o n o n	_____	8. o n o s
_____	2. c l i n u d e	_____	9. d T u s a y e
_____	3. n w e k	_____	10. o t
_____	4. o h t o t	_____	11. o w t
_____	5. c s a e s u i t	_____	12. o o t
_____	6. o o s h c e	_____	13. t r u i f
_____	7. f s d c o n u e	_____	14. d o f o

ACTIVITY 18 **Spelling Practice**

Write the word that you hear. You will hear each word two times.

1. _____ 6. _____ 11. _____

2. _____ 7. _____ 12. _____

3. _____ 8. _____ 13. _____

4. _____ 9. _____ 14. _____

5. _____ 10. _____ 15. _____

ACTIVITY 19 **Spelling Review: Which Word Is Correct?**

This review covers the different ways of spelling **u** in sch**oo**l in this unit. Read each pair of words. Circle the word that is spelled correctly.

	A	B		A	B
1.	Joon	June	11.	choose	chuse
2.	soap	soup	12.	joos	juice
3.	schul	school	13.	spoon	spune
4.	fruit	froot	14.	tru	true
5.	shoe	shu	15.	nun	noon
6.	blu	blue	16.	inclood	include
7.	Tuesday	Tusday	17.	do	du
8.	foud	food	18.	you	yu
9.	compoter	computer	19.	roule	rule
10.	noos	news	20.	muisic	music

Read the four words in each row. Underline the word that is spelled correctly.

	A	B	C	D
1.	scholl	school	schul	schule
2.	famos	famoso	femous	famous
3.	stret	estret	street	streat
4.	usually	usally	usully	usualy
5.	spon	spoon	spune	spoun
6.	bole	bowl	poul	powl
7.	shees	chees	sheese	cheese
8.	doctor	doctr	dactor	docter
9.	fainli	finali	finally	fainally
10.	Chainese	Chinese	Chineese	Chinees
11.	pipel	people	peeple	bebel
12.	Inglesh	Anglesh	English	Englis
13.	languaje	language	lenguaje	lenjuge
14.	classroom	classroon	clasroum	classroum
15.	frenly	frenli	frendly	friendly
16.	trebel	troble	truble	trouble
17.	practese	practes	practice	proctice
18.	estudent	estuden	studen	student
19.	imformation	imformetion	information	informetion
20.	reali	realy	really	realli

Original Student Writing

Writing Your Ideas in Sentences or a Paragraph

Write six to twelve sentences on your own paper. Write about a job or hobby that a family member or friend has. The job can be very good, very bad, or very interesting. Use the coordinating conjunctions **and, but, so**.

For help, you can follow the examples in Activity 11 and Activity 12.

Peer Editing

Exchange papers from the above activity. Read your partner's sentences.

Then use Peer Editing Sheet 3 on ELTNGL.com/sites/els to make comments about the writing.

PREPARING TO READ

BUILDING
VOCABULARY

A Read the questions. Choose the correct answers.

1. Which animal is **dangerous**?
   a. a kitten   b. a lion

2. Which are many people **afraid** of doing?
   a. flying   b. walking

3. Which is an outdoor **activity**?
   a. running   b. sleeping

4. Which has a **brain**?
   a. a house   b. a baby

BUILDING
VOCABULARY

B Use the words in **blue** to complete the sentences.

> succeed   goal   enjoy

1. I like running. I really _____ it.

2. I want to run five miles. That's my _____.

3. I can run five miles. I know I can _____.

USING
VOCABULARY

C Complete the information to make sentences about you.

1. One of my favorite activities is _____.

2. I enjoy this activity because it is _____.

3. I am afraid of _____.

4. My goal for this school year is to _____.

A ski jumper flies through the air during a tournament in Innsbruck, Austria.

LIVING ON THE EDGE •))) Track 9

Some people ski down mountains. Others photograph **dangerous** animals. Why do people **enjoy** risky **activities** like these?

THRILL SEEKERS

Taking risks makes some people feel good. Marvin Zuckerman is a psychologist. He says these people look for change and excitement. New or risky activities make a chemical in the **brain**. This creates a nice feeling. These people love this feeling. They want to feel it often.

GOAL-DRIVEN RISK-TAKERS

Other people take risks to reach a **goal**. For example, Mike Fay is a conservationist. He went on a dangerous 2,000-mile journey in central Africa. He worked to save wildlife there.

PROFESSIONAL RISK-TAKERS

For other people, taking risks is part of their job. Shane Murphy is a sports psychologist. He says extreme athletes are different from most people. Danger makes them feel in control. The danger can even help them. Daron Rahlves is a skier. He says being **afraid** makes him try harder to **succeed**.

EVERYDAY RISK-TAKERS

Most of us are not extreme athletes or explorers. But we still take risks. Some of us take social risks. For example, we may talk to people we don't know at a party. Sometimes we take risks with money. An example is buying a house. And sometimes we take risks with work. For example, we may leave a job. Most people take risks in some ways, but not others. What kind of risks do you take?

UNDERSTANDING THE READING

GUESSING MEANING
FROM CONTEXT

A Circle the main idea of the text.

1. For some people taking risks is part of their job.

2. Taking risks makes some people feel good.

3. There are different reasons people take risks.

UNDERSTANDING
DETAILS

B Read the questions. Choose the correct answers.

1. Marvin Zuckerman is a _____.
   a. skier   b. psychologist   c. conservationist

2. New or risky activities make chemicals in the _____.
   a. heart   b. eyes   c. brain

3. Mike Fay went on a dangerous journey in _____.
   a. South Africa   b. Central America   c. central Africa

4. Danger helps Daron Rahlves _____.
   a. succeed   b. think   c. feel good

EXPANDING
UNDERSTANDING

C What kind of risk-taker are you? Check (✓) the kind. Write an example of the risk. Then tell a partner your example(s) of how you take risks.

I am a thrill seeker. I like skateboarding down big hills!

Kind of Risk Taker	Me	Example
1. thrill seeker		
2. goal-driven risk-taker		
3. professional risk-taker		
4. everyday risk-taker		

PREPARING TO READ

A Use the words in **blue** to complete the sentences.

> strong   without   surprisingly   trouble

1. People need water. We can't live _____ it.

2. I tried chocolate popcorn yesterday. It was _____ good!

3. My little sister broke the window. She is in _____ .

4. Elephants can carry 9,000 kg. They are _____ .

B Read the questions. Choose the correct answers.

1. Which letter **follows** F in the alphabet?

   a. E   b. G

2. Which country is **close** to France?

   a. Australia   b. Spain

3. Which is a **size**?

   a. small   b. shirt

C Answer each question with one word that is true for you.

1. I wear a size _____ shoe.

2. There is a _____ close to my home.

3. I can't live without _____ .

Ashima Shiraishi bouldering in Texas, U.S.A.

Brian Skerry's dive partner appears tiny next to a right whale.

RISK TAKERS ⋅))) Track 10

For some people, taking risks is part of their lives. Here are two examples.

TEENAGE ROCK CLIMBER

Ashima Shiraishi is still in high school. But she's one of the best climbers in the world. She goes bouldering. In bouldering, climbers climb rocks up to six meters high. They do it **without** any equipment. So they have to be very **strong**.

The least difficult climbs are level V0. The most difficult are level V16. In 2016, Shiraishi climbed a level V15 boulder called Horizon. She was 14. She was the second person to climb it. She was the youngest person, and the first female.

It is a dangerous sport. Shiraishi knows this. But she continues to climb in the most difficult places around the world. Why? She says: "My dream is to keep on pushing myself, and, maybe, I will push the sport itself."

UNDERWATER PHOTOGRAPHER

Brian Skerry is an underwater photojournalist. He travels around the world. He goes diving with dangerous sea animals. To get great photos, Skerry gets as **close** as possible.

Once in New Zealand, Skerry swam next to a right whale. It was the **size** of a bus. Skerry thought, "I've got to get this picture!" He swam after the whale, but he became tired. He stopped. **Surprisingly**, the whale stopped too. It waited for him. Then the whale began to **follow** him. "It was like swimming around with a friend," Skerry says. Why does he take these risks? He wants people to think about life in the oceans. He thinks his photos can help. He says, "The oceans are in real **trouble**. As a journalist, the most important thing I can do is to bring awareness."

UNDERSTANDING THE READING

A Circle the main idea of the text.

UNDERSTANDING MAIN IDEAS

1. Ashima Shiraishi and Brian Skerry take risks.

2. For some people, taking risks is part of their lives.

3. Bouldering is a dangerous sport.

B Read each statement. Circle *True* or *False*.

UNDERSTANDING DETAILS

1. Shiraishi is in high school.   True   False

2. Shiraishi was the third person to climb Horizon.   True   False

3. Skerry takes photos under water.   True   False

4. Skerry swam with a shark.   True   False

C Read each question. Circle *Shiraishi* or *Skerry*. Then use the sentence frame below to explain your choice.

EXPANDING UNDERSTANDING

I think Shiraishi / Skerry is (stronger / in more danger / having more fun) because

he / she _____.

1. Who do you think is stronger?   Shiraishi / Skerry

2. Who do you think is in more danger?   Shiraishi / Skerry

3. Who do you think is having more fun?   Shiraishi / Skerry

PREPARING TO READ

BUILDING
VOCABULARY

A Complete each sentence with the correct word.

1. Climate change is making the earth hotter. The earth's temperature is
   _____ . (**rising / falling**)

2. There are only about 740,000 elephants in the world. There are
   _____ one million elephants. (**under / over**)

3. In 50 years, there may be no elephants. Elephants are _____ .
   (**safe / in danger**)

BUILDING
VOCABULARY

B Read the questions. Choose the correct answers.

1. Which is a **temperature**?
   a. +75   b. 75°

2. Which country is **warmer**?
   a. Italy   b. Iceland

3. Which country is **cooler**?
   a. Russia   b. Brazil

USING
VOCABULARY

C Answer the questions.

1. Do you prefer cooler or warmer weather? _____

2. Are there over or under 10 students in your class? _____

3. Is the number of people in your town rising or falling? _____

An endangered baby green sea turtle

SEA TURTLES FEEL THE HEAT •)) Track 11

Sea turtles are one of the oldest animals in the world. There were sea turtles **over** 200 million years ago. But they are **in danger**. Their numbers are **falling** because of climate change.

Conservationists[1] think climate change affects[2] turtles in a few ways. First, **temperatures** are **rising**. This makes sea levels rise. This floods beaches. Sea turtles lay their eggs in beach sand. Floods can kill the eggs.

Also, more male turtles are born in **cooler** temperatures. The world is getting **warmer**. So there are more female turtles. Scientists are worried. Soon there may be no males.

But people are trying to help. Mariana Fuentes is a conservationist. She is trying to keep sea turtles **safe**. She says, "To give marine turtles a better chance, we have to protect their nesting sites." There are now projects around the world. These projects help protect[3] turtle eggs from other animals and from humans. Conservationists also move eggs to cooler, safer areas.

There are some successes. In the early 1990s, there were fewer than 5,000 green sea turtle nests in Florida. Conservation work helped. By 2015, there were just **under** 30,000. But Fuentes believes the turtles still need help. She says, "Turtles were here long before humans. It would be a complete tragedy[4] if they were to become extinct[5] as a result of our actions."

[1] A **conservationist** is a person who works to help the environment.
[2] The weather **affects** the clothes we wear.
[3] If you **protect** something, you keep it safe from harm.
[4] A **tragedy** is something very sad.
[5] An **extinct** animal is not living anymore.

UNDERSTANDING THE READING

UNDERSTANDING
MAIN IDEAS

A Circle the main idea of the text.

1. Sea turtles are one of the oldest animals in the world.

2. Soon there may be no male turtles.

3. Sea turtles are in danger because of climate change.

UNDERSTANDING
DETAILS

B Read each statement. Circle *True* or *False*.

1. There were sea turtles over 200 million years ago.	True	False
2. Climate change makes sea levels rise.	True	False
3. There are more female turtles born in cooler temperatures.	True	False
4. There were over 5,000 sea turtle nests in Florida in the early 1990s.	True	False

EXPANDING
UNDERSTANDING

C Write three things you learned about sea turtles from the reading. Write three things you want to know about sea turtles.

I learned: *Sea turtles are in danger.*

I want to know: *Is the number of sea turtles rising now?*

Sea Turtles	
I Learned:	**I Want to Know:**
1.	1.
2.	2.
3.	3.

QUICK READ UNIT 3 READING 2: *Animals in the Frame*

PREPARING TO READ

A Use the words in **blue** to complete the sentences.

BUILDING VOCABULARY

> disappear   shocked   fortunately   unfortunately

1. Mario won $1,000 dollars! He was _____ !

2. I'm tired. _____ , it's almost bedtime.

3. I'm hungry. _____ , the refrigerator is empty.

4. The keys were here. Now they're not. How did they _____ ?

B Read the questions. Choose the correct answers.

BUILDING VOCABULARY

1. Which is a part of **nature**?

   a. trees   b. phones

2. Which must we **save** from disappearing?

   a. computers   b. endangered animals

3. Which do people usually **care about** more?

   a. their hair   b. their family

C Circle the answers that are true for you. Talk to a partner about your answers.

USING VOCABULARY

1. Which do you care about most: friends / family / money? Why?

2. Imagine you can save one of these animals. Which do you want to save: turtles / elephants / lions? Why?

3. Which is your favorite place in nature: the beach / the forest / the mountains? Why?

◄ **A bison poses for a Photo Ark photo. Sartore uses either white or black backgrounds for his photos.**

ANIMALS IN THE FRAME))) Track 12

Joel Sartore is a **nature** photographer. He uses his camera to **save** endangered species[1]. His photos tell the stories of these animals.

Sartore is working on a project. It is called Photo Ark. There are photos from the project on pages 53–55. What is the goal of the project? It is to take photographs of as many animals as possible before they **disappear**.

Q How did you become interested in saving endangered species?

A When I was a child, I read about Martha, the very last passenger pigeon. Martha died in 1914. I was **shocked**. In the past, there were 5 billion passenger pigeons—probably more than any other bird. But here was the last one, and there was no way to save it. How did we let this happen? I couldn't understand it. I still feel the same way. I want to stop this from ever happening again.

Q How does photography help to save endangered species?

A Photography is the best way to show problems to the world. It gets people to **care** about the problems. It's not enough to just show pretty animals in beautiful places. Now we must show the dangers to these animals as well.

Malayan tigers are endangered. Sartore says, "We tried photographing him on a big black background, but he just destroyed it. He looked like he really enjoyed it, too!" **Fortunately**, the tiger was OK with white paper.

Sartore took the photo of an eagle on page 54 at a zoo in Madagascar. **Unfortunately**, this eagle is one of the most endangered birds in the world. The population in the wild is under 100.

The lemur leaf frog is another endangered animal. This kind of frog was common in South America ten years ago. But now there are 80 percent fewer of them.

This baby chimpanzee is called Ruben. Sartore says, "Ruben's mother left him, so people at the zoo are raising[2] him. While I took the photo, his caregivers were gently holding him. Baby primates are much like human children—they need a mother to hold on to, even if it's human."

---

[1] An **endangered species** is an animal or life form that is in danger of disappearing.
[2] Parents **raise** their children by giving them love, food, and education.

UNDERSTANDING THE READING

A Circle the main ideas of the text.

UNDERSTANDING MAIN IDEAS

1. Joel Sartore uses his camera to save endangered species.

2. There are 80 percent fewer leaf frogs than there were 10 years ago.

3. Joel Sartore is working on a project called Photo Ark.

B Read the questions. Choose the correct answers.

UNDERSTANDING DETAILS

1. What animal made Sartore interested in endangered species?
   a. passenger pigeons   b. leaf frogs   c. Malayan tigers

2. When did the last passenger pigeon die?
   a. 1940   b. 1914   c. ten years ago

3. What is one of the most endangered birds in the world?
   a. eagles   b. owls   c. passenger pigeons

4. Where was the lemur leaf frog common 10 years ago?
   a. North America   b. Central America   c. South America

5. How are baby primates like human children?
   a. They need mothers.   b. They need bananas.   c. They need a home.

C Complete the prompts in writing with your own ideas. Then discuss your ideas with a partner.

EXPANDING UNDERSTANDING

1. I think Sartore's work is / is not important because _____ .

2. I think taking photos of endangered animals helps / doesn't help because

_____

3. My favorite Photo Ark photo on pages 53–55 is the _____
   because _____ .

VOCABULARY EXTENSION UNIT 1

Some nouns can be made into adjectives by adding -ous. The suffix -ous means "full of."
For example, *poisonous* means full of poison. Follow these spelling rules:

For most nouns add -ous	poison—poison**ous**
For most nouns ending in -e, cut the -e and add -ous	fame—fam**ous**
For most nouns ending in -y, change the -y to -i and add -ous	mystery—myster**ious**

A Complete each sentence with the adjective form of the nouns below.

> adventure   danger   fame   mountain   vary

1. I am not very _____. I don't like high-risk activities such as skydiving.

2. Daron Rahlves is a(n) _____ skier. He won many races and also appeared in several movies.

3. There are _____ reasons why people take risks. One reason is that taking risks makes people feel good.

4. Most ski resorts are found in _____ areas of the world.

5. Skydiving can be a(n) _____ activity. Some people have died or been seriously hurt.

Here are some common nouns and adjectives that collocate with the word *size*.

average size	**class** size	**shoe** size
actual size	**right** size	**wrong** size

B Complete each sentence with one of the collocations from the box above.

1. As a teacher, my perfect _____ is about eight to ten students.

2. This is only a model. The _____ is three times bigger.

3. This shirt doesn't fit me. It's the _____.

4. Different parts of the world have different systems for measuring _____. For example, a size 11 in the United States is a 10.5 in the United Kingdom.

5. In 2013, the _____ of a new home in the United States was 50% bigger than in 1983.

VOCABULARY EXTENSION   UNIT 3

We use comparative adjectives to compare two things. For example:

*A car is **bigger than** a bicycle.*

Follow these spelling rules:

- For most one-syllable adjectives add -er. For words that end consonant-vowel-consonant, double the final consonant and add -er. For words ending in -e just add -r.

  *cool—cool**er***   *big—big**ger***   *nice—nice**r***

- For most two-syllable adjectives ending in -y replace the -y with -i and add -er.

  *busy—bus**ier***

- For most two- or three-syllable adjectives add *more*.

  *expensive—**more** expensive*

A Complete each sentence using the comparative form of the adjective in parentheses and *than*.

1. A chimpanzee is _____ (small) an elephant.

2. An elephant is _____ (heavy) a chimpanzee.

3. Surfing is _____ (adventurous) sitting on your couch.

4. Tropical areas of the planet are _____ (warm) polar areas.

5. Photographing animals in a studio is _____ (safe) photographing them in the wild.

We often use the preposition *about* to introduce a topic. It often follows a verb. For example:

*Let's **talk about** the problems you are having at school.*
*I **worry about** global warming. I think it's a big problem.*
*I often **think about** my grandma. I remember how kind she was.*
*We often **laugh about** all the silly things we did as kids.*
*For my next essay, I will **write about** endangered animals.*
*I **care about** what happens to the blue-throated macaw.*

B Circle the best collocation to complete each sentence.

1. Many people **laugh** / **worry** about global warming. They think it could have a bad effect on the planet.

2. In a recent article, *National Geographic Magazine* **wrote** / **thought** about the effects of global warming.

3. I saw my teacher after class and we **talked** / **cared** about my poor grade.

4. Most teachers **write** / **care** about their students. They want their students to do well.

5. Joel Sartore takes photos of endangered species to make people **laugh** / **care** more about them.

GRAMMAR REFERENCE

UNIT 1
Language for Writing: Simple Present Tense (Negative)

Be			Other verbs		
I	**am not** **('m not)**	happy. sad. here. at work.	I You We They	**do not** **(don't)**	**like** tennis.
You We They	**are not** **(aren't / 're not)**				
He She It	**is not** **(isn't / 's not)**		He She It	**does not** **(doesn't)**	

UNIT 1
Language for Writing: Adverbs of Frequency

Be				Other verbs		
I	am ('m)	**always** **usually** **often** **sometimes** **hardly ever** **never**	busy.	I You We They He She It	**always** **usually** **often** **sometimes** **hardly ever** **never**	eat(s) breakfast.
You We They	are ('re)					
He She It	is ('s)					

UNIT 3
Language for Writing: Present Continuous Tense

Affirmative			Negative		
I	am ('m)		I	am not ('m not)	
You We They	are ('re)	**listening.**	You We They	are not (aren't / 're not)	**listening.**
He She It	is ('s)		He She It	is not (isn't / 's not)	

Note: Use *will* for things that are certain. Use *might* or *may* for things that are uncertain.

EDITING CHECKLIST

Use the checklist to find errors in your writing task for each unit.

	WRITING TASK	
	1	2
1. Is the first word of every sentence capitalized?		
2. Does every sentence end with the correct punctuation?		
3. Does every sentence contain a subject and a verb?		
4. Do your subjects and verbs agree?		
5. Do all possessive nouns have an apostrophe?		
6. Are all proper nouns capitalized?		
7. Is the spelling of places, people, and other proper nouns correct?		

Brief Writer's Handbook

The Parts of a Paragraph

What Is a Paragraph?

A **paragraph** is a group of sentences about **one** specific topic. A paragraph usually has three to ten sentences.

A paragraph is indented. This means there is a white space at the beginning of the first sentence.

Here is a group of sentences that can also be a paragraph.

Sentences	Paragraph
1. I have a big family.	indent I have a big family. My name is Anna Sanders. I am twenty years old. I study English at my school. I have two brothers. I also have two sisters. I love my brothers and sisters a lot. We are a very happy family.
2. My name is Anna Sanders.	
3. I am twenty years old.	
4. I study English at my school.	
5. I have two brothers.	
6. I also have two sisters.	
7. I love my brothers and sisters a lot.	
8. We are a very happy family.	

Parts of a Paragraph

A paragraph has three main parts: the topic sentence, the body, and a concluding sentence. See the example below that shows these parts.

1. The Topic Sentence

Every good paragraph has a **topic sentence**. The topic sentence tells the main idea of the whole paragraph.

The topic sentence:

- is usually the first sentence in the paragraph.
- should not be too specific or too general.

If a paragraph does not have a topic sentence, the reader may not know what the paragraph is about. Make sure every paragraph has a topic sentence.

2. The Body

Every good paragraph must have sentences that support the topic sentence. These supporting sentences are called the **body** of a paragraph.

The supporting sentences:

- give more information, such as details or examples, about the topic sentence.
- must be related to the topic sentence.

A good body can make your paragraph stronger. You must be sure to cut out any unrelated or unconnected ideas.

3. The Concluding Sentence

In addition to a topic sentence and body, every good paragraph has a **concluding sentence**. This sentence ends the paragraph with a final thought.

The concluding sentence:

- can give a summary of the information in the paragraph.
- can give information that is similar to the information in the topic sentence.
- can give a suggestion, an opinion, or a prediction.

topic sentence   the body

I have a big family. My name is Anna Sanders. I am twenty years old. I study English at my school. I have two brothers. I also have two sisters. I love my brothers and sisters a lot.

concluding sentence (opinion)

We are a very happy family.

Read each paragraph and answer the questions that follow.

Example Paragraph 1

The Best Place to Relax

My back **porch** is my favorite place to **relax**. First, it has lots of comfortable chairs with soft pillows. I feel so good when I sit in them. My back porch is also very peaceful. I can sit and think there. I can even read a great book and nobody **bothers** me. Finally, in the evening, I can sit on my porch and watch the sunset. Watching the beautiful colors always calms me. I can relax in many places, but my back porch is the best.

a porch: a part at the front or back of a house with only a floor and a roof

to relax: to rest or do something enjoyable

to bother: to make someone feel worried or upset

Post-Reading

1. How many sentences are in this paragraph? _____

2. What is the main topic of this paragraph? (Circle.)

    a. The writer likes watching the sunset.

    b. The writer likes to read a book in a quiet place.

    c. The writer likes to relax on her back porch.

3. What is the first sentence of this paragraph? (This is the topic sentence.) Write it here.

    _____

    _____

4. The writer gives examples of how her porch is relaxing. List the four things the writer does to relax on her porch.

    a. ___The writer sits in comfortable chairs._____

    b. _____

    c. _____

    d. _____

5. Read the paragraph again. Find at least two adjectives and write them below.

    _____

6. Read the topic (first) sentence and the concluding (last) sentence of the paragraph. Write down the ideas that these two sentences have in common.

    _____

Example Paragraph 2

Taipei 101

  I work in one of the world's tallest buildings—Taipei 101. This building is in Taipei's business **district**. Taipei 101 opened to the public in 2004. It is made of **steel** and glass panels, so it has a beautiful silver color. It has 101 **floors**. There are even five more levels below the building! Many international businesses have offices in Taipei 101. There are great places to shop in the building, too. I am **proud** to work in such an important place.

a district: an area

steel: a very strong metal

a floor: a level of a building

proud: having a very happy feeling of satisfaction

Post-Reading

1. How many sentences are in this paragraph? _____

2. What is the main topic of this paragraph? (Circle.)

   a. information about a city

   b. information about a person

   c. information about a building

3. What is the first sentence of this paragraph? (This is the topic sentence.) Write it here.

   _____

   _____

4. Answer these questions in complete sentences.

    a. Where is the building?

    _____

    b. How old is the building?

    _____

    c. What color is the building?

    _____

    d. How many floors does the building have in total?

    _____

5. Read the paragraph again. Find at least four adjectives and write them below.

_____

6. Read the topic (first) sentence and the concluding (last) sentence of the paragraph. Write down the ideas that these two sentences have in common.

_____

Parts of a Paragraph: The Topic Sentence

Every good paragraph has a **topic sentence**. The topic sentence is one sentence that tells the main idea of the whole paragraph.

The topic sentence:

- is usually the first sentence in the paragraph
- should not be too specific or too general
- must describe the information in all the sentences of the paragraph

If a paragraph does not have a topic sentence, the reader may be confused because the ideas will not be organized clearly. Make sure every paragraph has a topic sentence!

ACTIVITY 2 Practicing Topic Sentences

Read each paragraph and the three topic sentences below it. Choose the best topic sentence and write it on the lines. Then read the paragraph again. Make sure that the topic sentence gives the main idea for the whole paragraph. Remember to indent.

Example Paragraph 3

Beautiful Snow?

_____ Snow is beautiful when it falls. After a few days, the snow is not beautiful anymore. It starts to **melt**, and the clean streets become **messy**. It is difficult to walk anywhere. The **sidewalks** are **slippery**. Snow also causes traffic problems. Some roads are closed. Other roads are **hard** to drive on safely. Drivers have more **accidents** on snowy roads. I understand why some people like snow, but I do not like it very much.

a. In December, it usually snows.

b. Some people like snow, but I do not.

c. I love snow.

to melt: to change from ice to liquid

messy: sloppy; dirty

a sidewalk: a paved walkway on the side of roads

slippery: causing a person to slip or slide, usually because of a smooth surface

hard: difficult

an accident: a car crash

Maria and Her Great Job

_____ She works at Papa Joe's Restaurant. She **serves** about 60 people every day. Maria can remember all the dinner orders. If there is a problem with any of the food, she **takes** it **back** to the kitchen **immediately**. Maria works very hard to make sure all her customers have a great meal.

a. My cousin Maria is an excellent server.

b. My cousin Maria works at Papa Joe's Restaurant.

c. Maria's customers do not eat big meals.

to serve: to give someone food and drink at a restaurant

to take back: to return

immediately: at that moment; very quickly

My Favorite City

_____ I love to see all the interesting things there. The city is big, exciting, and full of life. I always visit the Statue of Liberty and the Empire State Building. I also visit Chinatown. At night, I go to **shows** on Broadway. The food in the city is excellent, too. I truly enjoy New York City.

a. I like to see the Statue of Liberty and the Empire State Building.

b. New York is a very big city.

c. My favorite city in the world is New York.

a show: a live performance on stage

Parts of a Paragraph:
The Concluding Sentence

In addition to a topic sentence and body, every good paragraph has a **concluding sentence**. The concluding sentence ends the paragraph with a final thought.

The concluding sentence:

- often gives a summary of the information in the paragraph
- often gives information that is similar to the information in the topic sentence
- can be a **suggestion**, **opinion**, or **prediction**
- should <u>not</u> give any new information about the topic

ACTIVITY 3 **Choosing Concluding Sentences**

Read each paragraph and the three concluding sentences below it. Choose the best concluding sentence and write it on the lines. Then read the paragraph again. Make sure that the concluding sentence gives a final thought for the whole paragraph.

Example Paragraph 6

Monday

I hate Monday for many reasons. One reason is work. I get up early to go to work on Monday. After a weekend of fun and relaxation, I do not like to do this. Another reason that I do not like Monday is that I have three meetings every Monday. These meetings last a long time, and they are **extremely** boring. Traffic is also a big problem on Monday. There are more cars on the road on Monday. Drivers are in a bad **mood**, and I must be more careful than usual. _____

_____

extremely: very

a mood: a person's emotion at a particular time

    a. Monday is worse than Tuesday, but it is better than Sunday.

    b. I do not like meetings on Monday.

    c. These are just a few reasons why I do not like Monday.

Buying a Car

Buying a car **requires** careful planning. Do you want a new or a used car? This depends on how much money you can spend. Sometimes a used car needs repairs. What style of car do you want? You can look at many different models to help you decide. Next, do you want extra **features** in your new car? Adding lots of extra features makes a car more expensive. Finally, you have to decide where you will buy your car. _____

_____

    a. It is important to think about all of these things when you are buying a car.

    b. The most important thing is the kind of car that you want to buy.

    c. Will you buy your new car from a friend or a car dealer?

to require: to need

a feature: an option, such as a DVD player or tinted windows

Hanami

Hanami is a very popular Japanese tradition. Every spring, thousands of **cherry** trees bloom all over Japan. For two weeks during Hanami, friends and families gather in parks and the countryside to see the beautiful flowers and celebrate the end of their vacation time. People make lots of food and have huge picnics under the lovely trees. There is lots of music and dancing, and large groups of people walk through the parks together. The celebration often continues into the night, and there are **lanterns** everywhere to light the celebration. _____

_____

a. People like to be with their family and friends during Hanami.

b. Looking at flowers during Hanami is interesting.

c. This is truly a most beloved Japanese custom.

a cherry: a small red fruit

a lantern: a light with a decorative cover

Writing the English Alphabet

A a   B b   C c   D d   E e   F f   G g   H h   I i   J j

K k   L l   M m   N n   O o   P p   Q q   R r   S s   T t

U u   V v   W w   X x   Y y   Z z

✓ There are 26 letters in the English alphabet.

    5 are vowels: A E I O U

    21 are consonants: B C D F G H J K L M N P Q R S T V W X Y Z

✓ When **w** and **y** come after a vowel, these two letters are silent vowels: **saw, grow, play, toy, buy.**

✓ When **w** and **y** are at the beginning of a syllable, they are consonant sounds: **wake, wish, when, year, young.**

Definitions of Useful Language Terms

Adjective An adjective is a word that describes a noun.

Lexi is a very **smart** girl.

Adverb An adverb is a word that describes a verb, an adjective, or another adverb.

The secretary types **quickly**. She types **very quickly**.

Article The definite article is *the*. The indefinite articles are *a* and *an*.

The teacher gave **an** assignment to **the** students.
Jillian is eating **a** banana.

Clause A clause is a group of words that has a subject-verb combination. Sentences can have one or more clauses.

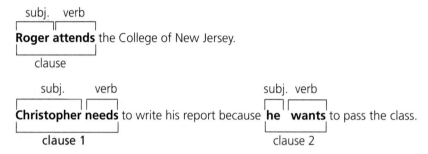

Noun A noun is a person, place, thing, or idea.

Sandra likes to eat **sandwiches** for lunch.
Love is a very strong **emotion**.

Object An object is a word that comes after a transitive verb or a preposition.

Jim bought a new **car**.
I left my **jacket** in the **house**.

Predicate A predicate is the part of a sentence that shows what a subject does.

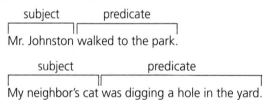

Preposition A preposition is a word that can show location, time, and direction. Some common prepositions are *around, at, behind, between, from, on, in, near, to, over, under,* and *with*. Prepositions can also consist of two words (*next to*) or three words (*in addition to*).

Punctuation Punctuation includes the period (.), comma (,), question mark (?), and exclamation point (!).

Subject The subject of a sentence tells who or what the sentence is about.

My science teacher gave us a homework assignment. **It** was difficult.

Tense A verb has tense. Tense shows when the action happened.

Simple Present:	She **walks** to school every day.
Present Progressive:	She **is walking** to school now.
Simple Past:	She **walked** to school yesterday.
Past Progressive:	She **was walking** to school when she saw her friend.
Simple Future:	She **is going to walk** to school tomorrow.
Simple Future:	She **will walk** to school tomorrow.

Verb   A verb is a word that shows the action of a sentence.

They **speak** French.

My father **works** at the power plant.

Review of Verb Tenses

Verb Tense	Affirmative	Negative	Usage
Simple Present	I work you take he studies she does we play they have	I do not work you do not take he does not study she does not do we do not play they do not have	• for routines, habits, and other actions that happen regularly • for facts and general truths
Simple Past	I worked you took he studied she did we played they had	I did not work you did not take he did not study she did not do we did not play they did not have	• for actions that were completed in the past
Present Progressive	I am working you are taking he is studying she is doing we are playing they are having*	I am not working you are not taking he is not studying she is not doing we are not playing they are not having*	• for actions that are happening now • for future actions if a future time adverb is used or understood
Simple Future (*Be Going To*)	I am going to work you are going to take he is going to study she is going to do we are going to play they are going to have	I am not going to work you are not going to take he is not going to study she is not going to do we are not going to play they are not going to have	• for plans that are already made • for predictions based on an action happening in the present
Simple Future (*Will*)	I will work you will take he will study she will do we will play they will have	I will not work you will not take he will not study she will not do we will not play they will not have	• for future plans or decisions that are made at the moment of speaking • for strong predictions • for promises/offers to help
Present Perfect	I have worked you have taken he has studied she has done we have played they have had	I have not worked you have not taken he has not studied she has not done we have not played they have not had	• for actions that began in the past and continue until the present • for actions in the indefinite past time • for repeated actions in the past
Past Progressive	I was working you were taking he was studying she was doing we were playing they were having*	I was not working you were not taking he was not studying she was not doing we were not playing they were not having*	• for longer actions in the past that are interrupted by other actions or events

Have can be used in progressive tenses only when it has an active meaning in special expressions, such as:

- *have* a party
- *have* a good time
- *have* a bad time
- *have* a baby

Capitalization Rules

1. The first word in a sentence is capitalized.

    I go to the movies every week.

    Deserts are beautiful places to visit.

2. The pronoun *I* is always capitalized.

    Larry and **I** are brothers.

3. People's formal and professional titles begin with capital letters.

    Mr. and **M**rs. Jenkins are on vacation.

    Lisa saw **D**r. Johansen at the bank yesterday.

4. Proper names (specific people and places) begin with capital letters.

    The **C**oliseum in **R**ome is a beautiful old monument.

    Kate met her brother **A**lex at the park.

5. Names of streets begin with capital letters.

    Ruth lives on **W**ilson **A**venue.

6. Geographical locations (cities, states, countries, continents, lakes, and rivers) begin with capital letters.

    I am going to travel to **L**ondon, **E**ngland, next week.

    The **A**rno **R**iver passes through **T**uscany, **I**taly.

7. The names of languages and nationalities begin with capital letters.

    My grandmother speaks **P**olish.

    Jessica is going to learn **J**apanese.

    Melissa is **V**enezuelan, but her husband is **C**uban.

8. Most words in titles of paragraphs, essays, and books are capitalized. The first letter of a title is always capitalized, and the other important words in a title are capitalized. Do not capitalize prepositions (*to, in*), conjunctions (*and, but*), or articles (*a, an, the*) unless they are the first word of the title.

    The Life of Billy Barnes

    Crime and Punishment

    The Catcher in the Rye

    In the Bedroom

9. Specific course names are capitalized.

    Nick is taking **H**istory 101 at 10:00 A.M.

    Nick is taking history this semester. (general subject—no capital letter)

Eight Common Comma Rules

1. Put a comma before *and, but, for, or, nor, so,* and *yet* when they connect two simple sentences. This creates a compound sentence.

    Rick bought Julia a croissant, but he ate it himself.

2. Put a comma between three or more items in a list or series.

    Jen brought a towel, an umbrella, some sunscreen, and a book to the beach.

3. Put a comma after a dependent clause (a clause that begins with a connecting word) when that clause begins a sentence. This is called a complex sentence.

> Because it was raining outside, Alex used his umbrella.

4. Put a comma before or after the name of a person spoken to.

> "Hamad, do you want to play soccer?" Ana asked.

> "Do you want to play soccer, Hamad?" Ana asked.

5. Commas separate parts of dates and places. Put a comma between the day and the date. Put a comma between the date and the year. Put a comma between a city and a state or a country. Put an additional comma after the state or country name if it appears in the middle of a sentence.

> I was born on Tuesday, June 27, 1992.

> The concert was in Busan, Korea.

> The headquarters of that company is located in Osaka, Japan.

> I lived in Phuket, Thailand, for ten years.

6. Use a comma to separate an introductory word or phrase from the rest of the sentence.

> Finally, they decided to ask the police for help.

> Every afternoon after school, I go to the library.

NOTE: *Then* is not followed by a comma.

7. Use a comma to separate information that is not necessary in a sentence.

> Rome, which is the capital of Italy, has a lot of pollution.

> George Washington, the first president of the United States, was a military officer.

8. Put a comma after the salutation in personal letters and after the closing in personal and business letters.

Dear Roberta,	Dear Dr. Gomez,	Dear Ms. Kennedy,
With love,	Sincerely,	Yours truly,
Grandma	Jonathan	Alicia

Spelling Rules for Regular Simple Present Verbs and Plural Nouns

1. Add -*s* to the base form of most verbs and to most nouns.

run	runs
work	works
love	loves

2. If a verb/noun ends in an *x*, *z*, *s*, *sh*, or *ch*, add -*es*.

box	boxes
buzz	buzzes
pass	passes
push	pushes
watch	watches

3. If a verb/noun ends in a consonant + *y*, change the *y* to *i* and add -*es*.

carry	carries
worry	worries
party	parties

4. If a verb/noun ends in a vowel + *y*, add -*s*. Do not change the *y*.

pay	pays
boy	boys
destroy	destroys

5. Add -*es* to *go* and *do*.

go	goes
do	does

Spelling Rules for Regular Simple Past Tense Verbs

1. Add -*ed* to the base form of most verbs.

start	started
finish	finished
wash	washed

2. Add only -*d* when the base form ends in an *e*.

live	lived
care	cared
die	died

3. If a verb ends in a consonant + *y*, change the *y* to *i* and add -*ed*.

dry	dried
carry	carried
study	studied

4. If a verb ends in a vowel + *y*, do not change the *y*. Just add -*ed*.

play	played
stay	stayed
destroy	destroyed

5. If a verb has one syllable and ends in a consonant + vowel + consonant (CVC), double the final consonant and add -*ed*.

stop	sto**pp**ed
CVC	
rob	ro**bb**ed
CVC	

6. If a verb ends in a *w* or *x*, do not double the final consonant. Just add -*ed*.

sew	sewed
mix	mixed

7. If a verb that ends in CVC has two syllables and the <u>second</u> syllable is stressed, double the final consonant and add -*ed*.

ad mit′	admi**tt**ed
oc cur′	occu**rr**ed
per mit′	permi**tt**ed

8. If a verb that ends in CVC has two syllables and the <u>first</u> syllable is stressed, do *not* double the final consonant. Just add -*ed*.

hap′ pen	happe**n**ed
lis′ ten	liste**n**ed
o′ pen	ope**n**ed

Irregular Simple Past Tense Verbs

These are some of the more common irregular verbs in English.

Base Form	Simple Past
be (am/is/are)	was/were
become	became
begin	began
bite	bit
bleed	bled
blow	blew
break	broke
bring	brought
build	built
buy	bought
catch	caught
choose	chose
come	came
cost	cost
cut	cut
do	did
draw	drew
drink	drank
drive	drove
eat	ate
fall	fell
feel	felt
fight	fought
find	found
flee	fled
forget	forgot
get	got
give	gave
grow	grew
have	had
hear	heard
hide	hid
hit	hit
hold	held

Base Form	Simple Past
hurt	hurt
keep	kept
know	knew
leave	left
let	let
lose	lost
make	made
pay	paid
put	put
read	read
run	ran
say	said
see	saw
sell	sold
send	sent
set	set
sing	sang
sink	sank
sit	sat
sleep	slept
speak	spoke
spend	spent
stand	stood
steal	stole
swim	swam
take	took
teach	taught
tell	told
think	thought
throw	threw
understand	understood
wear	wore
win	won
write	wrote

Possessive Pronouns

In general, possessive pronouns are used in spoken English. However, it is important to know how to use them. Possessive pronouns take the place of a possessive adjective + noun combination. In a sentence, a possessive pronoun can be a subject or an object.

Possessive Pronoun	Example
mine	That is not your book. It is **mine** (= my book).
yours (singular)	I don't have my pencil. I need to use **yours** (= your book).
his	My ring is silver, but **his** (= his ring) is gold.
hers	Carol has my cell phone, and I have **hers** (= her cell phone).
ours	Your room is on the first floor. **Ours** (= our room) is on the fifth floor.
yours (plural)	Our class got to have a special party. **Yours** (= your class) did not.
theirs	Jenny likes her class, and Karl and Jim like **theirs** (= their class), too.

Order of Adjectives

Adjectives can go before nouns. When more than one adjective is used before a noun, there is a certain order for the adjectives.

Example: He has a **brown** dog. It is an **enormous** dog.

✗ He has a brown enormous dog.

✓ He has an enormous brown dog.

In general, there are seven kinds of adjectives. They are used in this order:

1. size   *small, large, huge*

2. opinion   *beautiful, nice, ugly*

3. shape   *round, square, oval*

4. condition   *broken, damaged, burned*

5. age   *old, young, new*

6. color   *red, white, green*

7. origin   *French, American, Korean*

It is common to have two adjectives before a noun but rare to have three or more adjectives before a noun. When there is more than one adjective before a noun, follow the order above. The noun always goes last. Remember that this list is only a general guideline.

✗ a white Japanese small truck

✓ a small white Japanese truck

✗ a broken large dish

✓ a large broken dish

Quantifiers

Quantifiers give more information about the quantity, or number, of a noun. Quantifiers usually go in front of a noun.

Quantifier	Example
With Count Nouns	
one, two, three (all numbers) a few few many another several a pair of a couple of	**Several** students went to the school office. **Many** people wanted to leave the city. Ellie put **a few** coins in the parking meter.
With Non-count Nouns	
a little little much	There is only a **little** milk left in the refrigerator. We get too **much** homework every night.
With Count or Non-count Nouns	
some (quantity meaning *only*) any a lot of the other other	They got into **a lot of** trouble. Mrs. Jones has **a lot of** friends. Adam does not have **any** money.

The Prepositions *At, On,* and *In*

Prepositions express different ideas. They can indicate time, location, and direction. Remember that a preposition is usually followed by a noun (or pronoun).

Three very common prepositions in English are *at, on,* and *in.* In general, we use *at* with small, specific times and places, *on* with middle-sized times and places, and *in* with larger, more general times and places.

	Time	Place
Small	**at** 1:00 P.M.	**at** the bus stop
Middle	**on** Monday	**on** Bayview Avenue
Large	**in** July **in** spring **in** 2004 **in** this century	**in** Toronto **in** Ontario **in** Canada **in** North America

The Preposition *At*

Location: Use *at* for specific locations.

> Angela works **at** the First National Bank.
>
> I always do my homework **at** my desk.
>
> Joel met Jillian **at** the corner of Polk Street and Florida Avenue.

Time: Use *at* for specific times.

> My grammar class meets **at** 9:00 A.M. every day.
>
> The lunch meeting begins **at** noon.
>
> Cate does not like to walk alone **at** night.

Direction: Use *at* for motion toward a goal.

> My brother threw a ball **at** me.
>
> The robber pointed his gun **at** the policewoman.

The Preposition *On*

Location: Use *on* when there is contact between two objects. We also use *on* with streets.

> The picture is **on** the wall.
>
> He put his books **on** the kitchen table.
>
> Erin lives **on** Bayshore Boulevard.

Time: Use *on* with specific days or dates.

> Our soccer game is **on** Saturday.
>
> Your dentist appointment is **on** October 14.
>
> I was born **on** June 22, 1988.

The Preposition *In*

Location: Use *in* when something is inside another thing.

> The books are **in** the big box.
>
> I left my jacket **in** your car.
>
> Barbara lives **in** Istanbul.

Time: Use *in* for a specific period of time, a specific year, or a future time.

> I am going to graduate from college **in** three years.
>
> My best friend got married **in** 2006.
>
> Mr. Johnson always drinks four cups of coffee **in** the morning.
>
> We will meet you **in** ten minutes.

More Prepositions

Here are a few more common prepositions of location. Remember that a preposition is usually followed by a noun (or pronoun). In the chart, the preposition shows the location of the ball (in relation to the box).

Preposition	Example
in	The gift is **in** the box.
on	Marta's gift is **on** the table.
under	Pedro keeps his shoes **under** his bed.
above/over	Sheila held the umbrella **over** her head to stay dry.
between	The milk is **between** the eggs and the butter.
in front of	Mark was standing in **front of** the restaurant.
in back of/behind	My shirt fell **behind** my dresser.
across…from	There is a supermarket **across** the street **from** my house.
next to/beside	The mailman left the package **next to** the door.

Useful Connectors for Writing

Coordinating Conjunctions

Coordinating conjunctions are used to connect two independent clauses (sentences).

Note: A comma usually appears before a coordinating conjunction that separates two independent clauses. (An exception is when the two clauses are both very short.)

Purpose	Coordinating Conjunction	Example
To show reason	**for***	He ate a sandwich, **for** he was hungry.
To add information	**and**	Carla lives in Toronto, **and** she is a student.
To add negative information	**nor****	Roberto does not like opera, **nor** does he enjoy hip-hop.
To show contrast	**but**†	The exam was difficult, **but** everyone passed.
To give a choice	**or**	We can eat Chinese food, **or** we can order a pizza.
To show concession/contrast	**yet**†	The exam was difficult, **yet** everyone passed.
To show result	**so**	It was raining, **so** we decided to stay home last night.

*The conjunction **for** is not common in English. It may be used in literary writing, but it is almost never used in spoken English.

Notice that question word order is used in the clause that follows **nor.

†The conjunctions **but** and **yet** have similar meanings. However, **yet** is generally used to show a stronger contrast.

Many writers remember these conjunctions with the acronym **FANBOYS**. Each letter represents one conjunction: **F = for, A = and, N = nor, B = but, O = or, Y = yet,** and **S = so.**

Subordinating Conjunctions

Subordinating conjunctions are used to connect a dependent clause and an independent clause.

NOTE: When the sentence begins with the dependent clause, a comma should be used after that clause.

Purpose	Subordinating Conjunction	Example
To show reason/cause	because	He ate a sandwich **because** he was hungry.
	since	**Since** he was hungry, he ate a sandwich.
	as	**As** he was hungry, he ate a sandwich.
To show contrast	although	**Although** the exam was difficult, everyone passed.
	even though	**Even though** the exam was difficult, everyone passed.
	though	**Though** the exam was difficult, everyone passed.
	while	Deborah is a dentist **while** John is a doctor.
To show time relationship	after	**After** we ate dinner, we went to a movie.
	before	We ate dinner **before** we went to a movie.
	until	I will not call you **until** I finish studying.
	while	**While** the pasta is cooking, I will cut the vegetables.
	as	**As** I was leaving the office, it started to rain.
To show condition	if	**If** it rains tomorrow, we will stay home.
	even if	We will go to the park **even if** it rains tomorrow.

Useful Vocabulary for Better Writing

Try these useful words and phrases as you write your sentences and paragraphs. They can make your writing sound more academic, natural, and fluent.

Topic Sentences

Words and phrases	Examples
There are QUANTIFIER (ADJECTIVE) SUBJECT…	*There are* many good places to visit in my country.
SUBJECT *must follow* QUANTIFIER (ADJECTIVE) *steps to* VERB…	A tourist *must follow* several simple *steps to* get a visa to visit my country.
There are QUANTIFIER (ADJECTIVE) *types / methods / ways*…	*There are* three different *types* of runners.
It is ADJECTIVE *to* VERB…	*It is* easy *to* make ceviche.

Supporting Sentence Markers

Words and phrases	Examples
One NOUN…	*One* reason to visit my country is the wonderful weather.
Another NOUN… *… another* NOUN	*Another* reason to visit my country is the delicious food. The delicious food is *another* reason to visit my country.
The first / second / next / final NOUN…	*The final* reason to visit my country is its wonderful people.

Giving and Adding Examples

Words and phrases	Examples
For example, S + V. *For instance,* S + V.	My instructor gives us so much homework. *For example,* yesterday he gave us five pages of grammar work.

Concluding Sentences

Words and phrases	Examples
In conclusion, S + V.	*In conclusion,* I believe that my parents are the best in the world.
It is clear that S + V.	*It is clear that* Guatemala is the best tourist destination in South America.
If you follow these important steps in VERB + *-ING…,* S + V.	*If you follow these important steps in* fixing a computer, you will not need to call an expert.

Telling a Story

Words and phrases	Examples
When I was X, *I would* VERB…	*When I was* a teenager, *I would* go to the beach with my friends every day.
When I think about that time, S + V.	*When I think about that time,* I remember my grandparents' love for me.
I will never forget NOUN…	*I will never forget* the day I left my country.
I can still remember NOUN… *I will always remember* NOUN…	*I can still remember* the day I started my first job.
X *was the best / worst day of my life.*	My sixteenth birthday *was the best day of my life.*
Every time S +V, S + V.	*Every time* I tried to speak English, my tongue refused to work!

Describing a Process

Words and phrases	Examples
First (*Second, Third,* etc.), *Next,* … / *After that,* … / *Then* … *Finally,* …	*First,* you cut the fish and vegetables into small pieces. *Next,* you add the lime juice. *After that,* you add in the seasonings. *Finally,* you mix everything together well.
The first thing you should do is VERB…	*The first thing you should do is* wash your hands.
Before S + V, S + V.	*Before* you cut up the vegetables, you need to wash them.
After / When S + V, S + V. *After that,* S + V.	*After* you cut up the vegetables, you need to add them to the salad. *After that,* you need to mix the ingredients.
The last / final step is… *Finally,* …	*The last step is* adding your favorite salad dressing. *Finally,* you should add your favorite salad dressing.

Showing Cause and Effect

Words and phrases	Examples
Because S+ V, S + V. S + V *because* S + V. *Because of* NOUN, S + V. S + V *because of* NOUN.	*Because* I broke my leg, I could not move. I could not move *because* I broke my leg. *Because of* my broken leg, I could not move. I could not move *because of* my broken leg.
CAUSE, *so* RESULT.	My sister did not know what to do, *so* she asked my mother for advice.

Describing

Words and phrases	Examples
Prepositions of location: *above, across, around, in, near, under*…	The children raced their bikes *around* the school.
Descriptive adjectives: *wonderful, delightful, dangerous, informative, rusty*…	The *bent, rusty* bike squeaked when I rode it.
SUBJECT + *BE* + ADJECTIVE.	The Terra Cotta Warriors of Xian *are amazing.*
SUBJECT + *BE* + *the most* ADJECTIVE + NOUN.	To me, Thailand *is the most* interesting country in the world.
SUBJECT *tastes / looks / smells / feels like* NOUN.	My ID card *looks like* a credit card.

SUBJECT + *BE* + *known / famous for its* NOUN.	France *is famous for its* cheese.
Adverbs of manner: *quickly, slowly, quietly, happily…*	I *quickly* wrote his phone number on a scrap of paper that I found on the table.

Stating an Opinion

Words and phrases	Examples
Personally, I believe / think / feel / agree / disagree / suppose (*that*) S + V.	*Personally, I believe that* New York City should ban large sugary drinks.
VERB + *-ING should not be allowed.*	*Smoking* in public *should not be allowed.*
In my opinion / view / experience, S + V.	*In my opinion,* smoking is rude.
For this reason, S + V. *That is why I think that* S + V.	*That is why I think that* smoking should not be allowed in restaurants.
There are many benefits / advantages to VERB + *-ING.*	*There are many benefits to* swimming every day.
There are many drawbacks / disadvantages to VERB + *-ING.*	*There are many drawbacks to* eating most of your meals at a restaurant.
I prefer X [NOUN] *to* Y [NOUN].	*I prefer* soccer *to* football.
To me, VERB + *-ING makes* (*perfect*) *sense.*	*To me,* exercising every day *makes perfect sense.*
For all of these important reasons, I think / believe (*that*) S + V.	*For all of these important reasons, I think* smoking is bad for your health.

Arguing and Persuading

Words and phrases	Examples
It is important to remember that S+V.	*It is important to remember that* students only wear their uniforms during school hours.
According to a recent survey / poll, S + V.	*According to a recent poll,* 85 percent of high school students felt they had too much homework.
Even more important, S + V.	*Even more important,* statistics show the positive effects of school uniforms on student behavior.
SUBJECT *must / should / ought to* VERB.	Researchers *must* stop unethical animal testing.
I agree that S + V. *However,* S + V.	*I agree that* eating healthily is important. *However,* the government should not make food choices for us.

Reacting/Responding

Words and phrases	Examples
TITLE *by* AUTHOR *is a / an* (ADJECTIVE) NOUN.	*Harry Potter and the Goblet of Fire* by J.K. Rowling *is an* entertaining book to read.
My first reaction to the prompt / news / article / question was / is NOUN.	*My first reaction to the article was* anger.
When I read / looked at / thought about NOUN, *I was amazed / shocked / surprised…*	*When I read* the article, *I was surprised* to learn of his athletic ability.

Building Better Sentences

Being a good writer involves many skills including correct grammar usage, varied vocabulary, and conciseness (avoiding unnecessary words). Some student writers like to keep their sentences simple. They feel that they will make mistakes if they write longer, more complicated sentences. However, writing short, choppy sentences one after the other is not considered appropriate in academic writing. Study the examples below.

> The time was yesterday.
>
> It was afternoon.
>
> There was a storm.
>
> The storm was strong.
>
> The movement of the storm was quick.
>
> The storm moved towards the coast.
>
> The coast was in North Carolina.

Notice that every sentence has an important piece of information. A good writer would not write all these sentences separately. Instead, the most important information from each sentence can be used to create ONE longer, coherent sentence.

Read the sentences again; this time, the important information has been circled.

> The time was (yesterday.)
>
> It was (afternoon.)
>
> There was a (storm.)
>
> The storm was (strong.)
>
> The (movement) of the storm was (quick.)
>
> The storm (moved towards the coast.)
>
> The coast was in (North Carolina.)

Here are some strategies for taking the circled information and creating a new sentence.

1. Create time phrases to begin or end a sentence: yesterday + afternoon

2. Find the key noun: storm

3. Find key adjectives: strong

4. Create noun phrases: a strong + storm

5. Change word forms: movement = move; quick = quickly

   moved + quickly

6. Create place phrases: towards the coast

   towards the coast (of North Carolina)

   or

   towards the North Carolina coast

Better Sentence:

Yesterday afternoon, a strong storm moved quickly towards the North Carolina coast.

Here are some other strategies for building better sentences.

7. Use connectors and transition words.

8. Use pronouns to replace frequently used nouns.

9. Use possessive adjectives and pronouns.

Study the following example:

(Susan) (went) somewhere. That place was (the mall.) Susan wanted to (buy new shoes.) The shoes were for (Susan's mother.)

Improved, Longer Sentence:

Susan went to the mall because she wanted to buy new shoes for her mother.

Practices

Follow these steps for each practice:

Step 1: Read the sentences. Circle the most important information in each sentence.

Step 2: Write an original sentence from the information you circled. Remember that there is more than one way to combine sentences.

Practice 1

A. 1. (Tina) is my (friend.)

   2. Tina (works.)

   3. The work is at (Washington Central Bank.)

     My friend Tina works at Washington Central Bank. _____

_____

B. 1. There are boxes.

   2. The boxes are on the table.

   3. The boxes are heavy.

_____

_____

C. 1. Caroline attends classes.

   2. The classes are at Jefferson Community College.

   3. The classes are on Wednesdays.

_____

_____

D. 1. Tuscany is a region.

   2. This region is in Italy.

   3. This region is beautiful.

_____

_____

Practice 2

A. 1. There are books.

   2. The books are rare.

   3. The books are in the library.

_____

_____

B. 1. Drivers have more accidents.

   2. The accidents happen on roads.

   3. The roads are snowy.

_____

_____

C. 1. Aspirin is good for headaches.

   2. Aspirin is good for colds.

   3. Aspirin is good for pain.

_____

_____

Practice 3

A. 1. Charlie is a man.

   2. Charlie is my uncle.

   3. Charlie works hard in a restaurant.

   4. The restaurant belongs to Charlie.

_____

_____

B. 1. Tourists often ride boats.

   2. The boats are on the Seine River.

   3. Tourists do this at night.

   4. Tourists do this to see the Eiffel Tower's lights.

   5. The tower's lights are beautiful.

_____

_____

C. 1. Steven is in bed.

   2. It is early.

   3. Steven does this to be ready to work hard.

   4. He is doing this again.

   5. His work is the next day.

_____

_____

Practice 4

A. (Hint: Use a coordinating conjunction.)

   1. Chavez's family received money.

   2. There was very little money.

   3. People treated them badly.

_____

_____

B. (Hint: Use a coordinating conjunction.)

   1. My parents were not rich.

   2. My parents were always happy.

_____

_____

C. 1. This book gives us information.

   2. There is a lot of information.

   3. The book gives us the information now.

   4. The information is important.

   5. The information is about life in the fourteenth century.

_____

_____

Practice 5

A. (Hint: Use a coordinating conjunction.)

   1. Angela needs to buy some fruits.

   2. Angela needs to buy some vegetables.

   3. Angela is shopping at the farmer's market.

_____

_____

B. 1. Visitors are standing in line.

   2. There are many visitors.

   3. The visitors are also waiting to take pictures.

   4. The pictures are of themselves.

   5. There are ruins in the background.

_____

_____

C. (Hint: Use a coordinating conjunction.)

   1. Lisana is working.

   2. This company works with computers.

   3. Lisana does not have a computer engineering degree.

_____

_____

Practice 6

A. (HINT: Create a complex sentence.)

   1. First, Carmen arrives.

   2. Then Carmen will perform some dances.

   3. These dances will be formal.

   4. Carmen will do these dances with her friends.

_____

_____

B. (HINT: Create a complex sentence.)

   1. I go to the theater.

   2. The theater is on Broadway.

   3. I do this often.

   4. The reason I do this is that I live in New York.

_____

_____